OUT OF THE
OF THE
ROUGH

OUT OF THE ROUGH

AN INTIMATE PORTRAIT OF LAURA BAUGH
AND HER SOBERING JOURNEY

LAURA BAUGH

with Steve Eubanks

RUTLEDGE HILL PRESS®

Nashville, Tennessee

Published in Nashville, Tennessee, by Rutledge Hill Press®, 211 Seventh Avenue North, Nashville, Tennessee 37219.

Distributed in Canada by H. B. Fenn & Company, Ltd., 34 Nixon Road, Bolton, Ontario L7E 1W2.

Distributed in Australia by The Five Mile Press Pty., Ltd., 22 Summit Road, Noble Park, Victoria 3174.

Distributed in New Zealand by Southern Publishers Group, 22 Burleigh Street, Grafton, Auckland.

Distributed in the United Kingdom by Verulam Publishing, Ltd., 152a Park Street Lane, Park Street, St. Albans, Hertfordshire AL2 2AU.

Typography by Roger A. DeLiso, Rutledge Hill Press®

Library of Congress Cataloging-in-Publication Data is available.

ISBN: 1-55853-755-4

Printed in the United States of America

1 2 3 4 5 6 7 8 9—04 03 02 01 00 99

To the seven most wonderful people in the world:
my children—Chelsea, E. J., Haley, Robert, Michael,
Evita, and Jamie Lee, who live with Mom
one day at a time

CONTENTS

fOREWORD

WHEN I FIRST MET LAURA BAUGH at a celebrity pro-am, I found her to be a very pretty sixteen-year-old girl with a great golf game and a smile that lit up the golf course. I could see that she had the talent and bright personality that could make her a star and give a big boost to the LPGA Tour.

I was so impressed back then that I recommended to my business manager and associate Mark McCormack that he sign her up as a client. He took my advice and helped make her one of the best-known figures in women's golf. Laura and I subsequently worked together on several occasions. One time we did commercials for Japanese television that depicted us as man and wife. I don't think anybody believed that we were really married, but doing those commercials with her was a lot of fun.

While Laura did go on to considerable success in golf, I certainly had no inkling of what would lie ahead for her in her personal life—as a wife and mother, and today as a recovering alcoholic. What Laura has done to get herself, her family, and her professional career back on track should be an inspiration to men and women both in and out of golf. On the following pages, Laura has opened her heart for all to see. This book is a testimony to her character, her honesty, and her ability not only as a golfer but also as a person.

I suspect that the spark in her personality that enhanced her public image has also helped her a lot in her personal battles. She has survived and righted herself in circumstances that surely would have ruined the lives of persons without such inner strength. I know Laura still loves to compete on the golf course, just as I do, but in sharing her life so openly and fairly, she already has won as big a battle as anybody could face.

—Arnold Palmer

ACKNOWLEDGMENTS

IN SITTING DOWN TO TELL the story of my life, I didn't realize how much help I would need in recalling names, places, dates, times, and details of events that happened to me throughout the years. A world of thanks goes out to Mark and Betsy McCormack, my good friends, without whom I might not be alive, much less embarking on this newest journey. Also, I want to thank Mark Reiter, Jay Burton, and Alastair Johnston of IMG for their tireless efforts in bringing this project to reality. Others who contributed to this book who deserve immeasurable thanks include Hale Baugh, Hale Baugh III, Beau Baugh, Jim Ritts, John Tolson, Mindy Moore, Judy Rankin, Sandra Post, the Vossler family, and, of course, my coauthor Steve Eubanks. Also, a special thanks to Larry Stone and Mike Towle of Rutledge Hill Press for believing in me and helping me share my story.

To all the others who contributed to this project in big and small ways, I want to offer my heartfelt gratitude. And to the many anonymous recovering alcoholics who have helped me change my life, I owe more thanks than there are words in the English language. Because of all of them, I am able to share my life with you.

$\mathcal{I}$NTRODUCTION

AT 8:00 P.M. ON MAY 17, 1996, I am sure I had a wineglass in my hand. At that stage in my life, the glass had become a permanent extension of my arm. I was cooking in the open-air kitchen of my Orlando home, and I never cooked without drinking. A little wine for the fish, a little taste for Laura. A splash for the veal, a glass for Laura. One for the chicken, two for Laura. By that time every activity in my home included a drink as part of the program. Sit-ups, aerobics, weight training, listening to music—all better after a drink or two.

By May 1996, though, the workouts were fewer and the drinks more frequent. I drank all the time. Forty-five minutes without alcohol and my hands would begin to shake. An hour, and I was a nervous wreck. Two hours, and my eyes would roll back inside my head, my color would fade, and the seizures would come.

Wine and champagne were my drinks of choice. Somehow I believed that no matter how many blackouts I suffered or how many times I was rushed to the hospital, as long as I drank good champagne and expensive wine, I couldn't be a drunk. Drunks bought rotgut—cheap no-name bottles of goo with twist-off caps and warning labels. Good white wine and champagne were different. They had been a part of my life for as long as I could remember, even when I didn't drink. Champagne was served at the dinners and cocktail parties I was summoned to as an LPGA golfer. All the distinguished and well-heeled ladies and gentlemen who attended those functions partook. Drunks never drank *champagne.* It was a sophisticated drink, served on silver trays by men in tuxedos. Even though I did most of my drinking alone at home, I was still a sophisticated drinker, certainly sexier, funnier, happier, and a better person in every way after downing a couple of bottles.

Alcohol and I had an arrangement: It would give me what I needed to get through my days and nights, and as long as I could still play golf—or at the end, at least, practice for half an hour or so—I would remain in control. After all, I had been pregnant eight times in fourteen years, and I hadn't had a drop of alcohol while pregnant or nursing. I must have been in control. Drunks were the people you saw on benches, sleeping in cardboard boxes, or pushing shopping carts through parks. A mother and a professional athlete was not a drunk. Besides, it was just wine. I drank day and night, waking up every hour or so to fumble through the house searching for one of the countless minibottles I'd stashed in boots, golf bags, dresser drawers, and on closet shelves. But it was still only wine. How bad could it be?

I don't recall what I was cooking on that Friday, but it didn't matter. My husband and kids would go through the kitchen and find entire meals I'd prepared and then put away. Just because nobody ate them didn't mean I wasn't going to cook. I loved to cook—still do—although my memory of the process these days is far better than it was then. The kitchen was my domain, even though I rarely ate. My calories came in a bottle, and for days on end the only food I would ingest was a couple of scoops of ice cream. As any good drinker will tell you, ice cream acts as a coating agent so that when you throw up the alcohol you don't have to contend with the lingering acidic taste of partially digested

Chardonnay. It's like Maalox in reverse. A little ice cream helps the alcohol come up, then you can drink enough coffee to get yourself sober and lucid for whatever motion is required, then it's back to the bottle. I had six children at the time, so I cooked and cooked and cooked some more. Friends and family members would run across a pot roast in the pantry, or a chicken marsala that I'd prepared and then cached in a drawer. It was perfectly normal for me at the time.

I had rules, though, and one of those rules was no eating or drinking in the living room. It was tough enough to provide financially for a husband and six children as a professional golfer, plus clean the house, cook the meals, do the laundry, work out, travel, and drink; I didn't need to worry about someone spilling crumbs or, in this case, iced tea on my living room carpet. The final straw came for me on May 17, 1996—a Friday. Someone I love dearly carried a glass of tea into my living room, and took a sip while sitting on my couch. I was only ten feet away, cooking the latest Laura Baugh culinary masterpiece. This person had willfully refused to respond to my obnoxious alcohol-induced prodding throughout most of the afternoon and evening, and I was certain that this glass of tea was a passive-aggressive way of getting back at me. I walked around the counter— actually a chest-high bar that separates my kitchen from the living room—and with wineglass firmly in hand, I said, "I told you not to drink tea on the couch. Now, don't do it!"

Pointing was never a part of my tirades, but I could raise my voice with the best of the best. This was one of those times. I could also turn on my heels and dismiss someone with the kind of military precision that would have made my father, a West Point graduate, proud. While I don't remember it, I'm sure I turned on a dime after my proclamation and retreated back to the kitchen.

The blow to my head dislocated my jaw, and left me dazed for a moment. It didn't hurt right away, partly because of the shock factor, but mostly because of the huge quantities of alcohol I had ingested.

I'd been hit!

I knew what it was to be struck by someone. For a time, much earlier in my life, I'd been in an abusive relationship, and there were a few moments back in those days when I didn't know if I would live or die. All those memories came flooding back into my cloudy mind as I fell back against the refrigerator and held up my hands in a defensive posture.

"Whoa! What are you doing?" I shouted.

If there was an answer, I didn't hear it. I remember the darkness and the pain climbing over me in a slow wave. There was blood, but that wasn't unusual. I'd fallen and bled many times in the previous year. There had been nosebleeds, cuts, bruises, times when I'd passed out, fallen, and split my forehead, lip, cheek, or other vulnerable body parts. On one occasion my mother had propped me up in the shower trying to sober me up. Of course, I'd fallen and cracked my head on the tile floor. I almost drowned in the shower. Then there was the prolific nosebleed in Palm Springs, the mugging—or what I thought at the time was a mugging—in Phoenix, and the many, many incidents at home. Blood had become an acceptable part of my arrangement with alcohol, but this was different. I'd been hit, assaulted in my own home.

After a period of time—I had no idea how long—the world that was my kitchen spun back into view, and it dawned on me I must have blacked out. I gulped down a painful breath, and the urge to vomit almost overwhelmed me. After a few unfocused moments, I saw red liquid on the cream tile kitchen floor. Somewhere in the recesses of my brain, I realized that I needed help. I had to get out.

Numb from the alcohol and dazed from the beating, I stood up and staggered out a sliding glass door and into my driveway. It was dark, and I had no idea if I'd been out for ten minutes or five hours. All I knew was that it was sometime between 8:30 P.M. and 5:30 A.M., and I was bleeding.

My neighborhood is very quiet. Situated in an upper-middle-class area of Orlando between Arnold Palmer's Bay Hill Club and the posh Isleworth development where Tiger Woods, Mark O'Meara, and Ken Griffey Jr. reside, it has very little late-night activity in the area, and even less crime. I had provided most of the high drama in the neighborhood for the better part of a year, and this was certainly no exception. Half-conscious and with only a rudimentary recollection of where I was, I staggered through my yard and headed toward my neighbor's home, tripping over a sprinkler head and landing face-first in some freshly laid centipede sod.

Jane, my neighbor and friend for years, had become accustomed to my bizarre behavior, so it wasn't a great shock to her when I showed up on her doorstep, mud-caked, bloodied, drunk, and disoriented. I had walked into doors and fallen on every conceivable hard surface.

I knew something was wrong with my jaw, and I knew that if the police came, they would figure out how much I'd had to drink. I'd go back to the hospital for more detoxification, which meant more IVs, more suicide straps, more lectures on the evils of alcohol...blah, blah, blah. I just wanted to have my jaw examined and make sure nothing was broken, so I could go home and drink some more. Jane rounded up Bobby, my husband, and he drove me to the emergency room at Sand Lake Medical Center.

I don't remember if we spoke in the car on the way to the hospital, but by that time my conversations with Bobby Cole had become rote. Bobby would ask some superficial questions about what happened, how I felt, and how much I'd had to drink, and I would snip some curt responses, if I chose to answer at all. Our relationship had degenerated to the point where the smallest conversations usually escalated into big-time fights. I'd taken my wedding rings off almost a year before, but rather than engage him in any sort of confrontations about our problems, I decided to retreat to my wineglass and adjourn into my own little world. Bobby would often say, "It's like you're here, but you're a million miles away." That's exactly the way I liked it. My world included my kids and me, and no one else was invited.

As they always did when I visited Sand Lake Medical, the first order of business was a blood-alcohol test. This time my blood-alcohol level was 4.2, dangerously high for a woman who never weighed more than 110 pounds and kept her body-fat percentage athletically low. I told the emergency room personnel the same lie I'd told Jane, that I'd had a little too much to drink and fallen into a door. "I'm a small person, and I've had a little too much to drink. No, I don't have a problem with alcohol. How dare you think such a thing! I just drank a little too much."

My records were on file at Sand Lake, so of course they knew better. The nurses and doctors dutifully treated me for a dislocated jaw while keeping their eye-rolling to a minimum. A little pain medication and a little advice later, and I was on my way back home.

That's when the drinking got really serious. A scene awaited me when we returned to my quiet home in my quiet neighborhood, and I was in no mood for a scene. It had been a good hour and a half since my last drink; I'd been beaten; I'd tripped over a sprinkler; my jaw was dislocated; and my husband and mother were reacting poorly. They were both running around the house trying unsuccessfully to gain control of the situation, and when that didn't work, they began yelling at me and at each other. It was an ugly scene. Not only that, the kids were home, which meant they needed attention, and some sort of explanation why Mom had been in the hospital—again. It was all just too much. A bottle of champagne beckoned to me from my bedroom. Drinking with a dislocated jaw required some creativity, but I'd spent years honing my skills on that front. There were plenty of times when my hands shook so badly that I couldn't pour a drink into a glass, so I would create elaborate braces and levers out of plywood, golf bags, bicycle wheels, and whatever else happened to be lying around in the garage. Countless nights at three or four in the morning, I would lie on my back on the cold concrete floor and pour champagne into my trembling mouth from some stabilizing contraption I'd devised. This time I simply had to sit on the floor and angle my head just right. Swallowing was painful, but that was okay. Two liters did the trick. The shaking stopped, and I was ready to face my family.

Something wasn't right, though. My body wasn't rebounding the way it usually did from these kinds of episodes. Sure, there was pain, but I'd grown accustomed to pain. This was something different, like something bubbling up from inside. Bobby noticed it first.

"Laura, something's wrong with your head," he said.

"Now what?" I said. When I reached up and felt my scalp, I knew he was right. My head was expanding like a water balloon. Within minutes I had discolored welts popping up all over my body. I looked like some morphing monster from one of the cartoons the kids liked to watch. Then the blood came.

At first I thought I'd simply re-opened a previous wound or that I'd cut myself somewhere without realizing it. Then I saw that blood was gushing from my nose and mouth. Mom and Bobby hustled up some towels, but we couldn't stop the flow. Blood started oozing from my ears and from the corners of my eyes. It was everywhere, coming faster than we could mop it up. I had blood all over my face, my hands, dripping down my chin and onto my chest. I was bleeding from beneath my fingernails. Within an hour of my release from the Sand Lake Medical Center, we were back in the car on our way to the hospital again, only this time I hadn't been hit, hadn't fallen, hadn't been mugged, or blacked out. This time I was bleeding from every orifice, and I had no idea why.

This time, I was afraid.

✦ ✦ ✦

It's commonly called "bleeding out" by those few in the medical profession who will discuss it. Bleeding out is horrifying. Blood flows from every opening, including your toenails, fingernails, and eyes. It signals a major internal eruption. Victims of ebola bleed out as their organs are consumed by the virus. Some end-stage AIDS patients bleed out, but even that is rare. Most bleedouts are alcoholics suffering from malnutrition and cirrhosis of the liver. Almost all of them die.

Back at Sand Lake Medical Center emergency, I passed straight through the admissions desk and was carted to a bed. A crowd of emergency room doctors and nurses began poking and prodding, and mopping up blood. There was a critical tone in the air as various tests were ordered, and corresponding results came back. No one would tell me exactly what was wrong with me. I was leaking like a spigot all over the bed, the floor, and on every piece of equipment that came my way. They strapped me to the bed—standard procedure for detoxification under what they considered "dangerous" circumstances. I'd been buckled down many times, and each time it infuriated me more than the last.

What did they think? Did they think I was trying to kill myself? That was a laugh. I was absolutely, positively convinced I was not going to die, no matter how much I drank. Each time I had an episode that landed me in the hospital, I learned a little more. "Gee, I'll know not to do that again," I would tell myself. Every time I detoxed, I would say, "I'm never going through that again." So I would run, work out, get back in shape, hit golf balls, and work on my game. Soon I would say, "Gosh, a Caesar salad and a glass of champagne would be great. I've earned it. I've worked hard, supported my family, done what it takes. I owe it to myself."

After they stopped the bleeding, I was moved to intensive care. I could tell from the no-nonsense expressions, clipped chatter, and rapid responses that this wasn't an ordinary run-of-the-mill detox. The swelling had increased in my head and on my back. My hands looked like inflatable gloves, and dried blood was caked over most of my body.

"I need to see Dr. Johnson," I told one of the passing nurses.

She didn't respond.

"Dr. Johnson is my physician," I said slowly so she could get every word. "I need to see him. Call Dr. Johnson."

My personal physician for years, Dr. Johnson had been looking after my aches and pains ever since I moved from Palm Springs to Orlando. He was a great guy, and I never felt inhibited around him. He would shoot me straight when I needed it, and, by the same token, he wouldn't turn a small injury into a big thing. He'd detoxed me at Sand Lake after I'd gone on a holiday drinking binge one year with my family. Three days and two nights in the hospital with plenty of IV fluids and round-the-clock monitoring to make sure I didn't have a heart attack and I was screaming to get out. Dr. Johnson gave me a lecture on alcohol, and I swore to him it would never happen again. For a while it didn't.

Before long I was back in Sand Lake, back on the IVs, and listening, once more, as Dr. Johnson gave me another, sterner lecture on alcohol abuse and the dangers it presented to my body. I thanked him, explained I'd made an awful error, and promised him this would never, ever, not-in-a-million-years happen again. I convinced myself it was the truth. There was no way I would be back in the hospital for something as foolish as drinking too much. That was something I could control, or so I continued to tell myself. By the fourth time I was admitted to Sand Lake for detoxification,

Dr. Johnson refused to treat me. But this was different. Now, I was bleeding all over the place, swelling up like the Elephant Man, and my skin was turning nasty and unnatural shades of gray, crimson, and dusty rose. I needed a physician who knew my history—someone who knew me and who understood what a mistake I'd made.

"Did you hear me?" I demanded. "I need to see Dr. Johnson!"

"He's not coming," the nurse said. "He doesn't think he can help you."

I didn't want to confess I was scared, but I knew this trip was very, very different, and it wasn't just the view from the intensive care unit that made me think that way. Usually the nurses and doctors at the Sand Lake Medical Center smiled and started conversations with things like, "Well, how are we feeling?" or "What seems to be the problem here?" This time there was none of that. No one smiled or spoke, and very few people would answer my questions. To begin with, why couldn't I get cleaned up? The blood was finally beginning to clot and scab, which made me look even more beastly. When a fortysomething attending physician finally came by, I pleaded.

"Why can't I clean up?"

"Because your blood isn't clotting properly, and if we irritate the scabs, we could reopen the wounds and start the bleeding again."

Okay, I understood the last part of that, but I also wanted to know *why* my blood wasn't clotting the way it should.

"Ma'am, this is serious," he said. "Your platelet count is 40."

That didn't mean much to me at the time, but I later learned that a normal platelet count is 180, and most people die when it hits 50.

Still, I just wanted some reassurance. This was a detox, and I was going to be fine, right? "What do you mean *serious*?" I asked. "You can't die from it?"

"Oh yes, you can," he said flatly. "At any moment."

Those words hit me like a board. No more blackouts, no more memory lapses or heart stoppages, or retreating into my own little world. I could die...would probably die a bloody mess in the Sand Lake intensive care unit. My eyes rolled back in my head, and I leaned over and vomited, but I stayed awake and alert.

God, I was going to die. I had a better chance of dying than living. After all I'd done, after all I'd been through, I was going to die a drunk in the bowels of this Orlando hospital.

Oh, God, how did I get here?

OUT

OF THE

ROUGH

CHAPTER *1*

ORDINARY PEOPLE

HI, I'M LAURA, AND I'M AN ALCOHOLIC.

I repeat those words now with no reservation, hesitation, or shame, but it took many years, a lot of tragedies, and several raps on death's door for me to realize there was a demon out there called alcohol trying to kill me. Like virtually all who suffer from alcoholism, I never considered my drinking to be a problem, even when I could no longer sleep through the night without minibottles of wine by my bedside. I am also a professional athlete, a golfer on the LPGA Tour who was Rookie of the Year in 1973, who happens to be a mother of seven—a "record" among active players on our tour. The thought of being an alcoholic was completely foreign to me. Mothers of seven and professional athletes don't have those kinds of problems.

Everyone in my circle of friends drank socially. Drinking was normal, acceptable, even expected. As an active professional golfer, I didn't see anything wrong with indulging in a cocktail or two, or three, or six. I had earned it. One evening my good friend and fellow LPGA golfer Marlene Hagge and I were having wine with dinner when she looked at me and asked, "Laura, why can't you sip it? Why do you guzzle it?" I looked at her as if she had just beamed down from the starship *Enterprise* and said, "Because I can." Why drink at all if you're not going to do it right? Even after being strapped down in a hospital during detoxification, I still rationalized my bizarre behavior and dismissed any notion that I might actually have a problem. Maybe I had "a little trouble with occasionally drinking too much." But I could stop any time I wanted, just as I had done during every one of my pregnancies. I didn't have a problem.

That lie almost killed me more than once, but it wasn't the only one I told myself or those around me. I lied to everyone—friends, family, total strangers—and I took advantage of anyone and everyone who would let me. For the better part of a year, there were countless friends from the LPGA; from my agency, International Management Group (IMG); and from my family who did everything in their power to help me. Without fail, I abused their trust and used them to feed my addiction. After Marlene Hagge married Ernie Vossler (the Landmark developer who created such projects as PGA West and who was a lifelong friend), I would visit them in Palm Springs and misbehave in insane ways, as if I were saying to them, "This is just me. I don't have a drinking problem. I just like wine." But for reasons I can't comprehend, they stuck with me, as did people like IMG president Mark McCormack and his wife, Betsy, and, of course, my parents and my brothers.

Since embarking on my recovery, I've apologized for things I said and did during those times, and I've even apologized for many things I don't remember but I assume I said and did, given my pattern of behavior. By 1996 the bottle was everything to me. I would lie for it; probably (although it never came to this) steal for it; and, most certainly, abuse every relationship I had ever developed to get it. The bottle was my life, my thoughts, my reason for getting up, and my way of going to sleep at night. Everything in my life revolved around the next drink. By the end, I had devised elaborate contingency plans for how I was going to get my wine if Central Florida were ever hit by a major hurricane or if an invading foreign force ever occupied Orlando. Those were the thoughts that consumed me in the final stages of my denial.

My slide toward alcoholism was a slow one as I adjusted my life to fit alcohol's all-consuming schedule. Looking back, I think it's almost surreal that someone who had so much and who seemed so together could fall so spectacularly. Many of the incidents in my life are like scenes from a movie where the star makes the wrong choices, then rationalizes the consequences with a dismissive "fiddle-dee-dee." The episodes, the choices, and the decisions I made seem so illogical and unbalanced now; it's almost like it wasn't me. It couldn't have been me who did those things, or said those things, or experienced those things. But in the final analysis, it *was* all me. I created my own problems through the choices I made. Now that I have survived and thrived, and now that I am living a life of recovery, I can say without hesitation that what happened to me was a blessing from God. I have been given the gift of a second chance, and while one of the lessons of my recovery is that I'm never supposed to predict my future, I know that my life can be a lesson for others. My highs have been in the heavens, and my lows have been close to hell, but perhaps my experiences will help someone recognize and deal with addiction before it consumes and destroys everything.

✦ ✦ ✦

I did not touch a single drop of alcohol until after my twentieth birthday. It was a screwdriver (vodka and orange juice) ordered for me by a dinner date. I took one sip, shuddered, and pushed the glass to the center of the table. Drinking wasn't for me. It didn't fit with my workout schedule, my golf schedule, or my busy appearance schedule.

For my first twenty years on this planet, I didn't drink, I didn't date, and I wouldn't have known where to find illegal drugs if my life had depended on it. I was "innocent," what my daughter's generation would now refer to as "absolutely clueless." When it came to anything outside the narrow boundaries of schoolwork and golf, I was ignorant. That is not to say I wasn't reasonably bright—I was offered a full four-year academic scholarship to Stanford, and I had earned two years of college credit from Cal State Long Beach before my eighteenth birthday—but when it came to the more secular and subtle ways of the world, I knew so much less than the average girl my age growing up in Southern California that it was frightening.

Being out of touch in the late sixties and early seventies did have its advantages. I had no contact with drugs and no interest in the prurient temptations of free love that gripped my generation. I didn't know and didn't want to know anything about the bourgeois capitalists all the kids my age were railing against, and I didn't feel the least bit connected with anything hip, groovy, or far out. I played golf and I studied. That was it. Even though my picture had been in lots of newspapers and magazines and I had appeared on national talk shows and even in a couple of movies, the one award for which I was a shoo-in when I turned professional at seventeen was Golf's Most Naive Rookie.

The biggest misconception about me during those early years was that I was some sort of sex symbol out to revolutionize women's golf. I was called "the Charlie's Angel of Women's Golf." One writer even likened me to Helen of Troy, if you can imagine that. Dwayne Netland of *Golf Digest* wrote, "She seems to have everything. Youth, dazzling looks, a spontaneously gracious manner, and a golf game good enough to win the U.S. Amateur. No one on the women's professional tour can match her income, or draw galleries as large." I was flattered, but I was also dumbfounded by it all. Because I didn't look like most female golfers, there was a hailstorm of media hype after I won the U.S. Amateur at age sixteen. After I turned pro, my agents did a wonderful job of positioning me. I took full advantage of the attention, but I never really understood it. I was just a kid who played golf and who happened to be lucky enough and good enough to compete at the highest level at a very young age. I was an athlete and an adolescent who was, in the purist sense of the word, clueless.

Being out of touch in the late sixties and early seventies did have its advantages. I had no contact with drugs and no interest in the prurient temptations of free love that gripped my generation.

At the time I was being labeled a "bombshell" and "Golf's Golden Girl," I didn't know there was a life outside of golf. I certainly didn't try to package myself as some new-age wonder woman. I enjoyed being considered attractive then, just as I am still flattered when people compliment my appearance today, but a sex symbol? Even after I turned pro, I kept to myself and to my work, so much so that many of the other girls on tour thought I was aloof. Nothing could have been further from the truth. Naive, yes; aloof, never. I was just another girl who loved golf and who wanted to live the American dream.

At some point, however, someone (whom I've never met) wrote a rule (which I've never actually seen) that says women who are attractive, who wear makeup, and who work on their appearance are, for some reason, disqualified from consideration as serious athletes. I've never understood why looks and golf are mutually exclusive, but they were when I was a teenager. People's attitudes on the subject have only gotten worse in recent years. When I was growing up, for example, *Golf Digest* (in addition to its annual list of Top 100 Golf Courses) would annually name their Most Beautiful Golfer. I won that award as a sixteen-year-old, the same year I became the youngest winner in the history of the U.S. Women's Amateur. The *Golf Digest* recognition was quite an honor, plus they paid me two hundred dollars! Such an award would be considered politically incorrect these days. Hordes of protesters would probably picket the Trumbull, Connecticut, offices of the magazine for such an offensive, degrading, sexist, nothing-to-do-with-golf label.

Those same protesters would probably launch a letter-writing campaign to the *Los Angeles Times*. The late columnist Jim Murray wrote, "The tour has lots of people who can shoot 68, but they don't look like Laura. Laura looked like something out of a chorus line, but when she came out, the rest of the tour looked more like a chorus of prison matrons or tugboat captains. Some of them even wore felt hats and smoked cigars."

Even as a teenager I knew it was okay for a woman to be attractive and still compete at the highest level of her sport, regardless of the snickers and stereotypes. Here I am at age eighteen participating in my first pro tournament, the 1973 Lady Tara Classic in Atlanta. (CORBIS/BETTMAN-UPI)

Ouch! I guess that was meant as a compliment, but it didn't win me any friends among the other women on tour. Murray meant no harm by what he wrote, but by then I was so hypersensitive to the charge that I was more interested in my looks than in my golf game, even innocent references would send me over the edge. It was a round of golf, not a fashion show.

My coach and best friend—my dad—taught me very early on that the golf ball doesn't know what you look like, and it doesn't care. No amount of makeup can make you hit the golf ball better, and no glamorous camera angles can help you sink a twenty-foot putt. The game is hard, but it is rewarding, and in the end, the game itself is the great equalizer.

◆ ◆ ◆

When he grew up in the heartland of pre–World War II Omaha, golf wasn't as convenient for my father, Hale Baugh II, as it was for me. In an era when young men's only exposure to the game came from caddying, my dad, like many of the kids of his generation, regularly looped bags and shagged balls for older golfers. If they were lucky, the kids got to hit a couple of shots a day after all the practice balls had been retrieved, all the clubs had been cleaned, and all the adults had retired to the nineteenth hole.

My dad discovered his passion for golf there in Nebraska. His father, Jimmy Baugh, formally introduced him to the game. But my father's parents divorced when he was a year old—an unusual and often scandalous event in those days—so my dad didn't spend a lot of quality golf time with either his mom or his dad. While my grandfather retained custody of my father, he was busy making a living (and something of a name for himself) as a newspaper reporter with the *Omaha World Herald* and the *Omaha Bee News*. An aggressive, almost obsessive journalist, my grand-father was actually wounded when he got caught in the crossfire of a gunfight when police broke up a gambling ring. Jimmy Baugh worked the police beat in Omaha, and while he almost died from his injuries, the shooting earned him a number of journalistic awards in the Midwest. His celebrity eventually landed him on television, where he worked alongside a young upstart named Johnny Carson at WOW in Omaha. Because of my grandfather's busy career, my great-grandparents, Hale Baugh Sr. and Zoneta Baugh, attended to raising my father. They lived in Omaha with their son, the semifamous reporter, so it was easy for them to spend time with my dad.

My grandmother Laura Baugh stayed in Omaha and continued to have close contact with my father. When my grandmother was in her fifties, my father bought a home for her only a few miles from my childhood house in Florida. That's where she lived until she died. My grandmother died young, and while the reasons were always shrouded in mystery, I have since learned that she struggled for years to overcome various addictions to prescription medication. Such things were not discussed in the 1930s, 1940s, and 1950s. If my grandmother had known what I know today, she might have had a better chance at a longer, healthier, and happier life. It's a shame that many addictions in that era were simply swept under the rug. We know now that families are always hurt by covering for an addict. Not only does keeping the problem hush-hush encourage the addict to continue misbehaving, addictive behavior is a genetically inherited trait. Children and, in my case, grandchildren of addicts are genetically predisposed to addiction. It's not just "the crazy aunt" who drinks too much; it's probably the crazy aunt's children, grandchildren, and perhaps her nieces and nephews as well.

Father never saw his mother in any compromising or unusual states, but growing up as an only child (he has a much younger half-brother who is a surgeon in Austin, Texas) and raised by his grandparents, he never had much opportunity. He was too busy being an athlete, a farm boy, and a handsome young man who had ambitions that extended far beyond the plains of Nebraska. The war had ended, and Father had just graduated from high school. After spending a year studying engineering at nearby Iowa State, Hale Baugh II decided to spread his wings. He transferred to Columbia University, where he found just how different New York was from the farms of Omaha. Father rekindled his love for the game of golf. He played at the Ridgewood Country Club in New York, and it was there that his passion for the game exploded. He worked and played every possible hour until he had honed his game to a highly competitive level.

Then duty called. Even though he was already attending Columbia, Father took a competitive exam offered by Congressman Ben Jenson of Iowa. When he scored the highest on the exam, Father transferred his Iowa State and Columbia credits and accepted an appointment to the United States Military Academy at West Point. This young farm boy had matured into a strappingly handsome and athletically gifted cadet on the fast track to an engineering degree and an officer's commission, courtesy of the United States military. He still played golf whenever he could, and his game continued to improve.

One day during the summer, when he returned home from West Point, Father meandered over the bridge from Omaha into nearby Council Bluffs, Iowa, for a little R 'n' R. There, at the Crystal Pool, a hotbed of libidinous rituals in postwar Council Bluffs, my dad met a seventeen-year-old lifeguard named Sally Louisa Boyer.

Like my father's family, the Boyers were Scandinavian immigrants who possessed a hard midwestern work ethic and the kind of salt-of-the-earth conservatism that came with living through the depression. Herman and Anna Belle Boyer struggled through the 1930s. Food was scarce, and medicine was a luxury only the wealthiest could afford. Before Sally Louisa was born, Herman and Anna Belle had lost an infant son to a congenital heart defect, a blow that almost permanently devastated the family. Then after the birth of a healthy daughter, they struggled through economic hardships with their farm and a gas station they owned in Council Bluffs. Few people drove during the depression, and throughout most of World War II, gas and rubber were rationed. Making a living with a gas pump was difficult at best. It wasn't until Herman went into the printing business at the outbreak of the war that the family was able to secure themselves financially. They did modestly well after that—well enough that they bought a ten-unit apartment building in Long Beach, California. Like many other Scandinavian immigrants in the Midwest, they moved to the coast to retire—but the Boyers never forgot the depression and the lessons it taught them. They passed those lessons on to their daughter, and Sally Louisa did her best to pass those same lessons along to me.

My father related to the Boyers' values and history. Hale and Sally didn't discuss their common heritage or cultural symmetries that afternoon in Council Bluffs, though. "He came around the pool in his uniform and he was the handsomest man I had ever seen," my mom later recalled.

They were married on January 22, 1947. One year later, Sally gave birth to a boy, Hale Baugh III—my oldest brother.

By the time Hale was born, my father, who had graduated from West Point in June 1946, was distinguishing himself as a newly commissioned officer. A few months earlier, in late 1947, West Point's commander of the corps of cadets had announced that some of the academy's best athletes had been selected as candidates for the 1948 U.S. Olympic team. Among them was my dad. Although he had never received any formal training in Olympic competition, Father was chosen to represent America in the pentathlon, an event consisting of horseback riding, fencing, shooting, swimming, and running—all skills Father had acquired on the farm in Omaha or learned as part of his military training. Already involved with a new infant at home and his engineering studies and military training, my father spent every *spare* waking hour training as part of the U.S. Olympic team that traveled to London in the summer of 1948.

I sometimes wonder if his life would have been any different if he'd medaled in that Olympics. The Olympic experience was, at that time, the essence of amateur competition. My dad, like the rest of the members of the U.S. team, did other things for a living. No one outside the professional ranks trained for sports full-time. Because West Point attracted the top performing (and most disciplined) athletes, the academy was always a natural breeding ground for Olympic recruiters. Cadets expected nothing more than the honor of representing their country and collecting memories for a lifetime. My father got both.

Mom didn't travel to England with him, since doing so with a seven-month-old in 1948 was not encouraged. She stayed home, kept the house, and dutifully played her role as Mrs. Hale Baugh II. At that time, Sally Baugh was happy. Like many women of her era, she found her identity in her marriage, and she fell right into the mold of the perfect military wife, attending white-glove teas and keeping the house presentable for the neighbors—always. The social hierarchy of military family life suited her just fine. After all, my dad was the handsomest man she'd ever seen. She would probably be a general's wife someday, or so she assumed at the time. She never whined. When my newly commissioned father proceeded to flight school at Randolph Field in San Antonio, his wife followed him, caring for the family, keeping the house, and performing her duties as an officer's wife.

Father...never once led me to believe I was anything but a perfect gift from heaven. But I've known for years that he gave up his PGA Tour ambitions because of me.

Her attitude changed somewhat in 1950, however. Six days after President Harry Truman committed the United States to military action in the Korean conflict, my father departed for combat with the 307th Bomber Group. He flew forty-eight combat missions over North Korea in ten months. It was in Korea that my dad had his first taste of the buffoonery that can exist in the military. It was one thing to take inane, often degrading, orders from upper-classmen at West Point, but it was another thing to put people's lives at risk. Dodging antiaircraft fire over North Korea, Father watched as members of his squadron, some of whom had been with him at West Point and on the Olympic team, were shot down. While he accepted that losing men was a part of war, he began to ask questions about the motives and tactics of many of his superior officers, a big-time no-no in the military. Perhaps it was just his natural curiosity, but Father quickly realized that military "need to know" information didn't suit his personality. He knew he wasn't a candidate for a twenty-year military career, so after serving his country at home and abroad, he accepted an honorable discharge and began life as a civilian. My mother rejoiced. Father had survived Korea, and when he came home, he announced his intentions to leave the military. The young family was back together and soon, in 1952, my second brother, Beau, was born.

My dad never lost his passion for golf, even in Korea where, like the Hawkeye character in *M*A*S*H*, he would slip out between bombing runs and hit a few shots or play a couple of makeshift holes around the base. Returning stateside, he worked on his golf game incessantly at various military installations, earning a reputation as one of the better amateur players in the country. A group of businessmen from Palm Springs offered to provide financial backing so he could play the PGA Tour when his stint in the military ended. He seriously considered turning pro until a minor "accident" caused him to redirect his efforts: My mother became pregnant in 1954, this time with me.

Father has never been bashful about admitting I was an unexpected and somewhat ill-timed accident, but Mom is less forthcoming about the details and her motives at the time. Although she never admitted it, Mom wasn't excited about the prospects of tour life. Traveling with the military was one thing; there was a certain hierarchy that existed in that life, even among wives. But golf pros

One year old, all dressed up, and perhaps somewhere to go—maybe a day of shopping? (PHOTO COURTESY OF HALE BAUGH II)

in the midfifties were little better than glorified gypsies with no social status or infrastructure on which to fall back. Mom already thought of herself as something of a golf widow, but she believed that voicing those concerns would somehow be inappropriate. Instead, she got pregnant. Two kids, ages seven and four, were manageable on tour, Father assumed. He could play, and Mom could keep up with the two boys, who by that time were walking, talking, and feeding themselves. Three children just wouldn't work and Mom, who never admitted I was an accident, knew it. Father never brought it up, never said "what if," and never once led me to believe I was anything but a perfect gift from heaven. But I've known for years that he gave up his PGA Tour ambitions because of me. Instead of turning pro, he channeled his golf efforts in another direction. He was accepted to the University of Florida Law School and established himself as a key member of that school's prestigious golf team.

By the time I was born, our family was living in Gainesville, Florida, and my dad was attending law school and playing on the golf team. Mom continued to be a wife and mother, keeping the house and adjusting herself to the role of a future lawyer's wife. Those adjustments weren't exactly what she had planned for herself, and Sally Baugh wasn't exactly as blissful as she had been in the early days when the handsomest man she had ever seen swept her off her feet. She had found her identity through being Mrs. Hale Baugh, wife of a West Point graduate and army officer. Now that had changed, and Mom began to grapple with the new identity she would have to assume. As I was being christened, with future PGA Tour stars Tommy Aaron and Doug Sanders standing in as my godfathers, a simmering tension was beginning to brew in the Baugh household.

It would be years before it boiled over.

CHAPTER 2

FAMILY TIES

I CAN'T REMEMBER A TIME when I did not play golf. From the moment I was able to stand, my dad put a miniature golf club in my hands and led me waddling around the living room of our Gainesville apartment to swat balls between naps and diaper changes. From the beginning it never occurred to Hale Baugh that his daughter wouldn't play golf. On the night I was born, a less-than-enlightened doctor came out into the waiting room and said, "Well, Mr. Baugh, you don't have a golfer this time." To which my dad said, "So, is it a boy or a girl?"

The women's game hadn't taken off in those days the way it has since, and many male golfers still thought women should play golf between 6:00 and 6:15 A.M. and between 8:00 and 8:15 P.M. The rest of the time we should be home tending to the children or playing bridge with the girls. Thank God my father never thought that way. I played golf with him and my brothers from the time I was big enough to hold a club, and none of the males in my family treated me differently because I was a girl. They played to win, and so did I.

I don't remember Gainesville and the University of Florida, since my dad graduated from law school when I was three years old, but I have seen enough photographs to know that I was a regular player at the University Golf Course with Father, my brothers, Doug Sanders, Tommy Aaron, and the rest of the guys on the golf team. Girl or no girl, I was there, and I was going to play. When my little legs would no longer carry me around the course, Father would strap me to the back of his golf bag and stow me on a pull cart until I recovered enough to resume my game. By the time I was three, I could play nine holes and beat any toddler, male or female, who came my way.

After receiving his law degree, and with the tour no longer an option (even though he certainly had the game for it), Father did not immediately go into law. Instead, he indulged his love of flying and his engineering background to land a job at Boeing. Young Hale was ten, Beau was six, and I was three when we learned we were moving to Seattle. We thought the whole thing was great—exciting and adventurous. Mom packed up the house and said good-bye to her friends in Gainesville. She remained silent as the Baugh family took up residence in the Evergreen State of Washington.

Once in Seattle, we picked up our family activities right where we had left off in Florida. The house sat on five acres next to the airfield where the Boeing plant was located, so with some shovels and mowers he scrounged up from various places, Father built a three-hole golf course in our backyard, and we resumed our daily ritual. My brothers and I would start playing golf when the sun was high enough to see, we would break for lunch, pick up our afternoon rounds, and wait for Father to join us when he got home from work.

This is the first known golf photo of me, taken while we were living in Gainesville, Florida. I'm sandwiched between my brothers, Beau on the left side of the photo and Hale on the right. We look like we're being silly here, but we didn't goof off much when we were out on the golf course keeping score. (PHOTO COURTESY OF HALE BAUGH II)

The four of us would play until we couldn't see the balls any longer and it was time for bed. My mother would watch, sometimes even coming out to walk around with us, but she never played golf—not once.

That might not seem like a big deal for many families. After all, there are a lot of wives of golfers or parents of golfers who choose not to play golf. In my family, however, golf was all we did, which meant that my mother didn't participate in the single activity the rest of us played every day with passion.

When I say we played every day, I mean that we played every single day. If it rained, we would play when it stopped. It if didn't stop, we would play when it slacked off to a mild downpour. In cold weather we would put on stocking caps, and in the heat of the summer, we would pull out the shorts. When I got a little older, it dawned on me how odd it was that I never went to the movies or to the mall, and I never hung out by the soda stand with my girl-friends. Any time I would suggest such things to my father, he would say, "Nope, come on. We're going to play golf."

My family had something we did together every single calendar day, and for that we were enormously lucky. I remember walking around the golf course, my dad saying, "Come on, Laura, hit it again." I would hit a few golf shots, then venture off to the woods where I would play with pine cones, sticks, and whatever else happened to be lying around. In a few minutes I would hear, "Come on, Laura, aim at me." I was too small to see much of the hole, and most of the time I was in the rough, so my dad became my target. "Come on, Laura, just aim at me," he would say. And I would.

To this day, my dad insists on standing behind the green when he watches me play. As a four-year-old it was okay to hit it at him, because he was always in the center of the fairway. As a professional on the LPGA Tour, it's not okay to hit it at him, because he's standing in the gallery, usually twenty to thirty yards in the rough. Father kept statistics of the fairways and greens I missed, the direction I would miss them, and where he happened to be standing at the time. Sure enough, if he was standing on the right side of the landing area, I was likely to miss the fairway to the right. If he was on the left side of the green, I would pull the ball left. Somewhere in the recesses of my mind, I still heard him say, "Come on, Laura, aim at me." Now when he watches me play, he either stays out of sight or he stands right behind the flagstick. "Come on Laura, aim at me, now!"

◆ ◆ ◆

We were already golf junkies by the time Boeing transferred my father to Cocoa Beach, Florida. A move back to warm weather, sandy beaches, and Florida golf courses had all of us leaping for joy. Plus, it was an incredibly exciting time to be in Cocoa. The seven original Mercury astronauts—all crew-cut, dapper, and as American as apple pie—were placed on a national pedestal, and Cocoa Beach, a sleepy little pine-tree town of low-rise ranch houses, brick-hard beaches, and cinder-block motels, had become a boomtown of rockets, astronauts, engineers, and everything that goes with a multibillion-dollar national project. The new word *aerospace* was being introduced into our language, and Boeing was on the cutting edge of that industry. Father was part of the team they wanted in Cocoa, and we were ecstatic. Golf, sunshine, beaches, and astronauts awaited us, and I'm sure the three Baugh children bounced every mile of the trip, asking, "Are we there yet?" at each state line from Oregon to Florida.

Mom again packed up the house, said good-bye to her friends, and made the trek almost three thousand miles across country. This time, though, she looked forward to the move. There was no place more center-of-the-universe exciting than Cocoa Beach in 1959, and we were smack in the middle of it.

My dad made three trips back and forth from Seattle to Cocoa, once driving with us, and two more times by air, flying his single-engine Cessna and his Piper Cub down to the beach. His love of flying was eclipsed only by his passion for golf, and he always owned at least one private airplane. With Father in transit and Mom setting up a new house and enrolling all of us in new schools, we were relegated to backyard golf for the first couple of weeks we were in Florida. But in no time, Father joined Cocoa Rockledge Country Club (now called Rockledge Country Club) and we were back on the golf course.

Soon we were into a rhythm in Cocoa. I would go to Panetta Elementary School in the morning and Cocoa Rockledge Country Club in the afternoon. Every couple of months the school would organize a field trip to Cape Canaveral where we ate peanut butter and jelly sandwiches while Alan Shepard, Gus Grissom, John Glenn, Scott Carpenter, Wally Schirra, and Gordon Cooper were launched into space. Afterward, I would go home and wait for my dad to return from work, so we could all go out to the golf course.

With opportunities blasting off faster than the rockets in and around Cocoa Beach, Father decided it was time to put his University of Florida law degree to work, so he quit Boeing and joined forces with his law-school buddy Jim Driscol. The two formed Driscol, Baugh, and McGraw, P. C., and his career as a lawyer began in earnest. I believed then, and I believe to this day, that my dad practiced law to free up more time for golf. After he left Boeing, we teed off earlier and stayed later, never missing a day, all day on weekends.

Father devised a game for us he called "the cod fish" game, loosely based on the game the Lost Boys played in

Never Land with Peter Pan. I would play the forward tees, my brothers would play the middle tees, and my dad would play the back tees, and we would compete against each other. Sometimes we would play three-hole matches, sometimes nine-hole matches, and sometimes they went on all day. At the end, the loser had to stand up during dinner and say, "I am a cod fish." It was a fate worse than death for a little girl, so I would play as hard as I could. Father showed no sympathy. Even though I was his little princess in all other circumstances (I was always the one who got the pre-dinner candy or the second scoop of ice cream), on the golf course I was just another competitor. And if I lost, I was just another cod fish.

At the end, the loser had to stand up during dinner and say, "I am a cod fish." It was a fate worse than death for a little girl, so I would play as hard as I could.

It drove my brothers nuts when I won, especially Beau—three years older than me and inclined to be wounded by his little sister beating him at anything. I was embarrassed to be the dinner-table cod fish, but Beau would sometimes dissolve into tears. I would say things like, "Sorry, Beau, I didn't hear you. Did you say you were Laura's cod fish?" His face would turn red and his lower lip would tremble, but Father wouldn't let him off the (proverbial) hook. If you lost, you were the cod fish. No exceptions.

By the time the summer of 1960 rolled around, at the ripe old age of five, I had been playing golf for three years. I was ready to take my game on the road. With Father at work, Mom gassed up our Volkswagen Beetle and drove my two brothers and me seventy miles west to Rio Pinard Country Club in Orlando for the National Pee Wee Invitational.

Although just eight years old at the time, I already had six years of golf experience under my belt en route to winning five National Pee Wee championships. (PHOTO COURTESY OF HALE BAUGH II)

Because of all the golf clubs and luggage, I had to sit on the back ledge of the Volkswagen with my clubs in my lap. But that didn't matter. As long as I was going to play golf, I would have clung to the roof.

For five years in a row I won the National Pee Wee in a trot. In the early years, I won by thirty or more shots—there weren't that many girls in the field—and I was the only one who had played since age two. At that time, most girls didn't pick up the game until they were ten or eleven years old. By then, I had five national victories.

Hale was a teenager, and he was winning most of the tournaments in his age group. Bob Murphy provided some serious competition for him, but Murph is older than Hale, so they weren't in the same age divisions very often. Beau, on the other hand, had some serious competition from a junior named Eddie Pearce from Tampa. A contemporary of Ben Crenshaw and Lanny Wadkins, Pearce played as well in those early days as any junior in the country, most of the time at the expense of my brother. So while I won most of the tournaments I entered in Florida—locally and nationally—and my brother Hale won most of his, Beau collected his share of trophies but lost to Eddie Pearce more often than not.

Throughout it all, my father continued to give each of us golf lessons, and, more importantly, he ferried us to the golf course every day. Even though his new law practice was working out nicely, things were not going well in the Baugh household.

The kettle that had been simmering for years suddenly blew its lid, and our lives would never be the same.

✦ ✦ ✦

I can't pinpoint exactly when my parents' marriage reached the point of no return. I remember the fights—name-calling and ugly accusations that escalated into brutal shouting matches—but I never really knew, and don't know to this day, what brought it all on. It was like one of the many rocket launches I'd watched out at the cape. There was a slow buildup, lots of preparation, and a countdown. Once the candle was lit, there was no way to stop it. My mom had been unhappy with my father, and her unhappiness soured into bitterness. Her bitterness soon festered, and before any of us knew what was happening, lamps were thrown, shouts were heard, and ugly, ugly scenes were repeated in our Florida home almost nightly.

Father did his best to keep the confrontations with Mom out of sight, but there was only so much he could do. His military background told him to control the situation, but when he attempted to calm things down, Mom would become even more enraged. How dare he raise his voice to her like she was some subordinate! She had given up her personal interests to take on the role of wife and mother, and now it was time for her to exert some control over her own life.

Even though he is only seven years older than I, my brother Hale virtually raised me from the fall of 1966 until late 1968; I call him Uncle Hale to this day. He made sure I completed my schoolwork, I had eaten properly, and I was protected from the feuding going on around us. By the time my father moved out the first time, I had resigned myself to the fact that Mom and Father were always going to fight. Uncle Hale was now in charge.

At least I still had golf. Not only was the club my respite from all the shouting and high drama, I found a sense of order and a measure of control on the golf course. Out there, with my balls and my clubs, I was in charge. I didn't realize it at the time, but the game was my escape mechanism—the world that I could retreat to, where I was still the master. Because of golf I was able to shut out most of what was going on around me, and as a by-product, I continued to improve my game.

Father moved into a small house a few miles from what we called "the Big House," although in hindsight I don't think it was that big. He and Mom tried several times to work out visitations, reconciliation, and terms on which they could peacefully coexist. None worked. I remember Father would sometimes bring groceries with him to the Big House, and my mother would say, "Great, you brought food, so now I have to cook it!" That sort of silliness would escalate into another fight, and before any of us knew what had happened, another full-scale scene erupted at the Baugh home. Mom's identity crisis had finally festered. Jumping from army wife, to law-student wife, to aerospace-engineer wife, to lawyer wife and mother had been too much. Sally Baugh didn't know what she wanted, but she knew she wasn't finding it as the wife of Hale II and the mother of Hale Jr., Beau, and me.

By late summer 1968 it was clear that the situation was untenable and divorce was imminent. I, for one, was ready. The scenes were just too much, and even as a twelve- and thirteen-year-old, I realized that anything was better than what we had. Once everyone came to the same realization, it was only a matter of working out the details. The Big House was put on the market, and my mother began making plans for the future.

My dad, a reluctant participant, simply wanted to ensure that he had contact with his children. By that time Hale was in college and Beau was sixteen years old, so my mother agreed to let the boys remain with my dad, but she insisted I was to live with her. My father knew that fighting for my custody would be futile. He agreed that Mom could keep me, with the provision that I remain in Florida. Mom's parents were in California by that time, and Father knew Mom was under some pressure to move to the West Coast.

For Father, California was unacceptable. His little girl was not going out there to that drug-infested concrete jungle, and he explained to my mother that not only would I be corrupted by drugs and crime and a morally lax lifestyle, he was convinced I would end up pregnant as a teenager, and my golf would be over. At least if we remained near Cocoa, he could keep an eye on me, and I could still play golf at Cocoa Rockledge with him and my brothers.

After much wrangling, on the morning of September 28, 1968, my parents divided their assets and finalized a divorce agreement where I would remain with my mother under the condition she would not move out of the state of Florida. So much for contractual law. On the morning of September 29, my mother sold most of our belongings and loaded the rest in a 1966 GTO. By that afternoon we were on the road headed for California and a brand-new, remarkably different life.

✦ ✦ ✦

My mom now openly admits that her motivation for taking me to California was to hurt my father. As a thirteen-year-old child, I had no idea. This was another adventure…a cool journey into the unknown. Mom drove straight through from one coast to the other while I fumbled through the road maps we picked up along the way.

When we finally arrived, road-weary and covered in grime, my grandparents put us up in one of the vacant units in their apartment complex. The reunion was short-lived. My grandparents loved us, but they also believed in personal responsibility, and they were not about to grant us a permanent entitlement program. They explained to my mother that rent for the apartment would be eighty dollars a month—substantially discounted from what they would have charged any other tenant. Mom pitched a fit, and within a few weeks, we had rented an apartment on Olive Avenue in Long Beach for forty dollars a month.

A two-story complex, the Olive apartment building looked like some of the seedier motels I'd seen on the roadside in what was then the undesirable section of Cocoa. When we pulled into the parking lot in our GTO, the first thing I noticed was people—hanging around the parking lot, lying on cars, standing on the corners, and sliding in and out of view from around the corners of the building. We were the only Caucasians anywhere in sight. A sea of black faces turned in our direction as this blonde Scandinavian woman and her even blonder thirteen-year-old daughter began hauling boxes up the rusted metal staircase and into the one-bedroom flat that looked out over the south parking lot.

The principles of sacrifice my mother had learned from her parents during their depression-era struggles were applied in force while we lived at Olive. No phone, no television, and no club membership. We got by with one bedroom, a small living area, an even smaller bath, and what would be classified a kitchenette in most middle-class areas of America. Our bathtub (we didn't have a shower) and sink both had old-time double faucets—one for hot and one for cold. I can still hear the squeaks of the handles and the rumble of water laboring through lead piping, and I can remember the smell of potatoes baking in a partially opened oven. For most of my junior high and high school years, we would bake potatoes for breakfast and crack the oven door to heat the apartment. I would eat lunch at school, then on the way home I'd stop off at Omega's and pick up a couple of Omega burgers at two-for-a-buck.

I became a voracious reader and exceptional student during that time, primarily because I was afraid to go out at night and we didn't own a television or a telephone. It was either read every night or engage my mother in lengthy philosophical discussions. I chose to read and study and within the first week of my tenure at Jefferson Junior High School, I was skipped a grade.

I didn't miss much time on the golf course, though. Because of my father's fervent conviction that I would end up pregnant and strung out on drugs if I moved to California, my mother was determined to prove him wrong. Even though she didn't play, she was not about to let my golf game slip because of the circumstances. We had no money, no club affiliation, and no contacts, so for the first nine months we lived in California, every afternoon I would dress like a boy and put my hair up. My mother and I would then sneak out to the third hole of Recreation Park Long Beach Golf Course where I would play, illegally.

Soon we discovered a small legion of like-minded kids who wanted to play golf but who didn't have the money. There were always about eight to ten of us who would sneak onto the public courses in foursomes. I was the youngest by at least three or four years and the only girl, but the guys didn't mind. A young girl turned out to be a great asset. When we got caught (which happened at least once every other day), my job was to cry. It never worked, but usually within a few minutes of being escorted from the premises, we were back out in the fairway trying to finish a couple of holes before being caught and kicked out again. Our record for expulsion was four times in one day. Each time I would dutifully lower my head, tremble my lip, and just as the burly park officer was saying, "You kids need to get out of here," I would start sobbing and gasping, covering my face and quivering as I raised and lowered my shoulders with each heaving breath. It was Academy Award stuff, but we still got the boot.

After a while we could anticipate when we were becoming conspicuous, so we alternated between Recreation Park Golf Course, Sky Links, and El Dorado, all public golf courses in the Long Beach area. We knew exactly where to start so we wouldn't be seen and exactly what times we were least likely to be noticed. If we were caught, I would cry, we would get booted, and then we would venture to the next course in the rotation.

Although all the guys in our group were older, I quickly earned their respect, mostly because of my golf game, but partly because I was the grandest misfit of the bunch. My mother actually chaperoned me on the course every day. The other kids were at least sixteen and driving, so while their parents might have some vague notions of the scams they were running by sneaking onto golf courses without paying, my mother was actually there, walking every step and watching every shot. It was just fine that I had sneaked onto a public golf course dressed as a boy with strict instructions to cry if we were caught, but God forbid I fraternize with a group of sixteen-year-old boys without my mother present.

The first couple of times it was strange, and every time a new kid joined our little band the questions were always the same. "That's your mom? You mean your mom sneaks out here with you?" I would explain that yes, indeed, it was my mother, and yes, in fact, she did sneak out with us every day. After a couple of stares, the response was always, "Hey, that's cool." Mom took a maternal interest in my new miscreant friends, pulling them aside and asking them about their girl-friends or their plans for the weekend. It was bizarre, but it was the only way I could continue playing, and it was an experience I wouldn't trade for anything in the world.

Fortunately, I didn't have to spend my entire junior golf career sneaking onto public courses. A year later, after I had nestled into a comfortable, albeit spartan routine, my mother took me to San Clemente to play in the Long Beach Junior Championship, one of the most prominent junior tournaments in the city. Early on I had discovered that Southern California had a much stronger junior golf pro-gram than Florida, but because I was slipping onto public courses with boys three to five years older than I, I was a complete unknown outside my rascally little band.

I might as well have been from Mars as far as the other girls were concerned. I looked different, dressed differently, sounded different, and definitely came from a different neighborhood. Most mothers escorted their daughters to the golf course, so we weren't odd in that respect. But once they arrived at the club, all the other moms either left and came back later, or they adjourned to the clubhouse for coffee and conversation. Not my mom. Just as she did when we were sneaking onto Recreation Park, she walked every step of the golf course and watched every shot I took. When I won the event by five shots, she couldn't have been happier. She had proven her point to my dad. We had been in California a full year, and not only had I *not* gotten pregnant nor fallen into moral decay, I had skipped a grade in school, earned straight A's, and had won the Long Beach Junior Championship at fourteen. Mom drew vindication with each breath. She had been right, and he had been wrong. The world was good.

The rest of the moms, along with the other girls in the field, all of the officials from the Southern California Golf Association, and a smattering of local reporters who covered the event were stunned by my victory. This was not supposed to happen. Amy Alcott was the queen of girl's junior golf in the region. She was supposed to win the Long Beach Junior, and every other junior championship in the area. Not only had I upset the established pecking order in the state, I was poor and my mother followed me around the golf course all the time! It was a travesty.

The car we drove, my choice of clothing, my hairstyle, even my propensity to play without socks, all became fodder for snickering girls.

For months I was known in junior circles as "that Florida girl." You know, the one who beat Amy Alcott in the Long Beach Junior; the one who spent a year sneaking onto public golf courses without paying; the one whose mother is with her every step of every tournament. The girls were cruel and catty, and the more I won, the crueler and cattier they became. The car we drove, my choice of clothing, my hairstyle, even my propensity to play without socks, all became fodder for snickering girls. I had to become thick-skinned very quickly, because I certainly didn't make many friends. At least I didn't have to sneak out to play any more. As one of the perks for winning the Long Beach Junior, I received free passes to all the Long Beach public golf courses. After that, my job was to get a legitimate tee time by myself and play the first hole alone so my friends could sneak onto the second hole and join me. At least one of us was legal, and even though the girls didn't think too much of me, at least I had the guys.

As I moved into high school, another uproar nearly cost me my male golfing buddies. When I was a freshman at Woodrow Wilson High School, my mom thought it would be wonderful if I played on the school golf team. That way I could compete in organized matches and get a lot more exposure throughout the state. The only problem was, like most high schools at the time, Woodrow Wilson didn't have a girl's golf team. That was all my mom, a burgeoning feminist, needed to hear.

After we moved to California and the divorce was finalized, my mother quickly shed the housewife image she had carried for two decades and embraced the California feminist movement with all her might and will. She even changed her name, insisting she be called Louisa instead of Sally. Later she would drop Baugh and insist that she was Louisa Boyer. Then later, Louisa Boyer-Baugh. Then Sally Louisa Boyer-Baugh. Mom became a spunky advocate for causes ranging from the ERA to Title IX. By the time I showed up for homeroom my freshman year of high school, she was a full-fledged, bra-burning, Gloria Steinem–disciple feminist. Establishing a girl's golf team at Woodrow Wilson High became her *cause du jour*. She campaigned to the principal, the superintendent, and the school board. She petitioned, lobbied, wrote letters, and organized protesters, all in the name of justice and equality for girl's golf.

I was mortified. All of a sudden "that Florida girl" was stirring up trouble with the school board. Even my friends, the guys I'd been playing golf with since arriving in California, started looking at me differently. The last thing I wanted or needed was to become a cause. Even the press picked up on it, putting my name and, of course, Mom's new name, right in the local news.

When a few savvy politicians on the school board came up with a compromise that made the golf team coed, I was really in a bind. Any girl who wanted to play could do so, but I was the only girl who wanted to play, and I was better than any of the boys on the team. Now, in addition to being a troublemaker, I was going to humiliate all the boys in my school by insisting I play on their golf team. *Oh by the way, I'm the best player in the school, so I'll be the number-one man on the team.* Thankfully, after more than a few confrontational discussions with me on the subject, my mom didn't demand that I follow through with playing. I wasn't about to be the poster girl she wanted, so, after her semivictory, she let the matter drop and moved on to other causes.

That same year, I won the Long Beach Women's Amateur, which opened more opportunities for me to play the courses throughout the region. Later that summer I won the Los Angeles Women's Amateur at Rancho Park, the course where the Los Angeles Open was held at the time. The Los Angeles Women's Amateur was the biggest tournament you could win in the state besides the California State Women's Amateur, so I was thrilled. All of a sudden I wasn't just "that Florida girl" any more. I had proven that I was as good as or better than any woman in the state, many of whom were three times my age. Along with Amy Alcott, future LPGA players like Debbie Meisterlin, Barbara Barrow, Jane Renner, and Leslie Spalding all played in the same California tournaments and all would agree that winning the Los Angeles Women's Amateur was a big, big deal. For me, at the ripe old age of fourteen, the most important aspect of the victory was that I could now play *all* the public courses in the city without having to pay. I was overjoyed. Finally, my days of sneaking in were over. I was legitimate.

It didn't occur to me at the time that I was too young to be winning. I thought I should win every time I played regardless of the event or the caliber of the field. So the next year, 1970, as I was sitting in the airport waiting on a student-standby pass to fly to Muskogee, Oklahoma, I was certain that I was about to win the United States Women's Open Championship at age fifteen. After all, my dad was going to be there, and I hadn't seen him in almost two years. I always played well with Father around. This was going to be a great reunion, maybe, I hoped, leading to a reconciliation between my mother and my father. If I played well enough, I reasoned, they would get back together.

✦ ✦ ✦

Whenever I was with my dad, it was like we had never been apart. When we were apart, though, it was like he was a total stranger. He couldn't call, because we didn't have a phone. For a long time I never understood why Father never came to California to see me, or why he didn't put up more of a battle when my mom moved us out of Florida in violation of the divorce decree. Later, I learned that attempting to get a contempt order in a civil divorce when one of the parties is twenty-five hundred miles away is like trying to will a mountain to move. Nor did Father have any allies

Beau and I are enjoying the lighter side of life somewhere out on the road while I'm competing in another amateur tournament, age fifteen. (PHOTO COURTESY OF HALE BAUGH II)

on the West Coast who would have supported visitation. Mom had sufficiently spun her side of the story to anyone and everyone who would listen, including her parents, so I'm sure Father thought that coming out to visit would ignite yet another scene, and that was the last thing anybody wanted.

Muskogee was our chance, though. The 1970 U.S. Women's Open was being played at Muskogee Country Club in the tumbleweed plains south of Tulsa, and Mom and I were meeting Father and my brothers there for the week. This was going to be it. This was my chance to bring the family back together.

When we arrived in Muskogee, Father was already there. He had booked two hotel rooms at a Holiday Inn and we stayed right next to him and my brothers. It was just like the old days, the good old days, before the fights, the name calling, and the scenes. Mom didn't scream or throw any melodramatic fits, and Father didn't raise his voice. It was going to work out.

The practice rounds were uneventful. The rest of the field averaged twice my age, and the wind blew constantly, but that was no big deal. I had beaten older players before, and there was no reason I couldn't do it now. We all had to play the same golf course, so the harder the wind blew, the better it was for me. I also remember all the USGA people being kind and helpful, especially future executive director Frank Hannigan. He went out of his way to make me feel comfortable and welcome, and as time went on, I realized how special that was. I had other concerns. My mom and dad were following me, but I didn't see much progress on the reconciliation front. They weren't fighting, but they weren't actually together either. If I could just win the tournament and go home U.S. Open champion, they would have to get back together. It was destiny.

A 74 in Thursday's opening round put my delusions of destiny just where they belonged. I hadn't played poorly, but the golf course was hard, and the competition was, well, U.S. Open caliber. Still I held out hope. I was on track to make the cut.

On Thursday night I thought our fortunes had changed. Mom and Father went outside together, and when I sneaked a look out the hotel room window, I saw them walking together around the pool. They were talking, not fighting. Their body language seemed civil enough. I felt sure something wonderful was going to happen. My fantasies were just that—fanciful longings of an emotionally charged fifteen-year-old. My parents didn't fight in our presence, but that didn't mean they were getting back together. I never found out what they discussed that night by the pool. I still wonder.

The next day I shot 78 and missed the cut by one shot. I cried, not so much because I didn't win the U.S. Open, but because I had failed my one chance to reconcile my family.

Donna Caponi won the Open that year with a four-day total of 294. It was her second consecutive Open victory and quite a historic accomplishment. My mother and I returned home to Long Beach, where I went back to Woodrow Wilson High School and began taking college courses offered through Cal State Long Beach. I didn't see my father again for another year.

CHAPTER *3*

*I*NSTANT FAME

THROUGHOUT MY AMATEUR CAREER, the USGA always scheduled the U.S. Junior Girls Championship and U.S. Women's Amateur in the same region of the country and within a couple of weeks of each other. That was particularly important when you were playing on a tight budget. In 1970, for example, both events were in New York over two consecutive weeks, and I was able to fly student-standby and stay with my aunt, Barbara Jacobellis, in Fairfield, Connecticut. Without that kind of arrangement, we probably couldn't have afforded for me to travel to both tournaments.

In the summer of 1971, the U.S. Junior Girls was held in Augusta, Georgia, and the next week, the USGA moved 150 miles west to Atlanta for the U.S. Women's Amateur. I was one of the favorites for the U.S. Junior Girls, but even more exciting was the fact that I got to fly east a week early to spend a few extra days with my dad in Cocoa Beach.

Although I flew out of LAX with no plans to return home for at least three weeks, I didn't check a bag, and I arrived at Father's house with no suitcase. I had the clothes on my back and my golf clubs, and nothing else. Mom had concluded that one way to update my wardrobe without her spending any money was to send me to Father's with nothing but my golf bag and a smile. At the time I didn't realize how calculating that little maneuver was on Mom's part, but there had been other incidents where my mother had finagled money out of Father with me as an unwitting accomplice. Whenever I wanted to send a letter to Father, for instance, the stamp had a price. I needed to ask for more money at least once in every letter for it to be mailed. I don't know if my requests were honored. Nor did I understand why I had traveled across the country with no clothes. But Mom knew.

After exchanging hugs and tears at the airport, Father and I headed to the mall for some serious shopping. Although we had a wonderful time and spent a small fortune at Dillard's, I felt sorry for my dad. When Mom and I had packed up and headed to California, I was a thirteen-year-old little girl with awkward teeth and a prepubescent body. When I returned to stay with him in Cocoa that week, I was a 118-pound, sixteen-year-old young woman who looked twenty. We had to buy everything—underwear, outerwear, socks, and sundries—and Father hadn't shopped for women's clothing in many, many years. To complicate matters further, I hated the "old lady" fashions that most girls wore on the golf course. I didn't want to dress like a man, so we had to get creative. Much later, when I was designing my own line of women's sportswear for David Crystal, I carried that same philosophy into the clothes I designed for others. On more than a few occasions, I laughed out loud on David Crystal's New York design floor as I remembered that day of shopping with my dad, recalling all the grunts, groans, and obligatory chants of "Yes, Laura. Whatever you want, dear." It was a wonderful day.

After a long search throughout most of the stores in the Cocoa Beach mall, Father and I settled on several sleeveless Izod dresses that were not considered classic golf attire but looked great and worked well. Little could I have known what an impression my fashion selections would make on the national media just two weeks later.

Our shopping spree complete, Father and I returned to our old stomping grounds at Cocoa Rockledge where we hit balls, worked on my swing, and played. Growing up I never had a teacher other than my dad—in California we couldn't afford lessons—and after almost three years of no instruction, my swing was long overdue for a tune-up. For five straight days Father and I hit balls and played while the sun was shining, then we ventured out for prime rib at night. I ate steak every night for two weeks and, in hindsight, the protein really helped me. While my standing in the California golf world had improved in the two years since I first started sneaking onto Long Beach public courses, my diet still consisted of baked potatoes, salad, and an occasional Omega burger. I never told Father what a treat the steak dinners were, but I think he sensed that I needed some good, hearty nourishment before a tough two weeks of competition. By the time Father and I loaded up in his Chevrolet and drove north on I-95 toward Augusta, I was well dressed and well fed, and my game was in good shape for the weeks ahead.

I had never been to Augusta prior to playing in the U.S Junior Girls Championship, and I was a little surprised by the town itself. Coming from Florida and California where golf courses were springing up faster than mushrooms, I assumed Augusta would be a haven for golfers and golf courses. That wasn't the case. There were a few private clubs, including the impressive Augusta Country Club where we were playing, but it was nothing like what I'd seen in Florida and California. During one of the early practice rounds, a group of us strolled through the right rough on the eighteenth fairway and wandered onto the twelfth green at Augusta National, right in the heart of Amen Corner. A few of the girls were concerned, but I was an old pro at sneaking out on golf courses, so I became the de facto leader of our little bunch. We didn't hit any shots, but we walked around the eleventh, twelfth, and thirteenth holes, taking in all the sights and sounds of one of golf's greatest venues. At the time I wasn't overly impressed, partly because I hadn't yet attended a Masters Tournament and didn't understand or appreciate the history of the place. As a sixteen-year-old, I was much more interested in Augusta *Country* Club and the tournament I was supposed to win.

After grinding through the medal rounds and winning my first two matches, I progressed to what everyone considered the key match of the tournament against two-time defending champion and Savannah native Hollis Stacy. Hollis was a year older, and she had a home-crowd advantage, as well as momentum from two previous U.S. Junior Girls Championship victories. When she won in 1969 at age fifteen, she became the youngest winner in the event's long history—a mark that still stands today. The night before my semifinal match, Father and I went out for another night of prime rib and starch. Although neither of us mentioned it, we both knew this was the most important round of golf I had ever played.

Still working on that follow-through at sweet sixteen, preparing for the California Junior Girls Championship. (Laura Baugh)

Hollis and I were both nervous the next morning, and the match seesawed back and forth early. On the back nine, however, I settled in and began winning holes, and by the time we reached the sixteenth tee, I was two holes up with three holes to play. While I knew I didn't have the tournament won just yet, I liked my chances, especially after hitting the sixteenth green in regulation. Hollis made a par, so all I had to do was two-putt for par and the match would be dormie. Hollis couldn't win in regulation; I couldn't lose.

In my amateur days, and for a number of years as a professional, I was an aggressive putter, often running my first putts past the hole as much as four or five feet if I didn't make them. As long as I was making the four-footers coming back, it wasn't a big deal. But with the pressure of competition, my short putting stroke sometimes failed. I made my share of putts, both long and short, but at that time the mechanics of my putting stroke were not so sound. I would often close the putter blade on my backstroke and open it on the forward stroke. If I timed it right, I putted well. If my timing was off just a little, I had problems.

Throughout that week and most of the summer, I had timed my putting stroke perfectly and putted well. With that in mind, I wasn't overly concerned when I ran my first putt on the sixteenth four feet past the hole. Then my timing failed me, and I missed my second putt. After reaching the green in regulation, I had three-putted! Instead of closing out the match on sixteen and advancing to the finals, or giving myself an opportunity to close it out with a halve on seventeen, I opened the door and curtsied for Hollis. As we walked to the seventeenth tee, I was only one up with two holes to play.

I was livid, and a flood of bad thoughts and old memories rushed through my mind. The previous December I had made it to the finals of the California Women's Amateur at Pebble Beach, where I was playing against future tour player Shelly Hamlin. The weather, as it often is along the Monterey Peninsula in December, was brutal, and it was a tough match. We fought the wind and cold and each other through thirty-six grueling holes, finishing the day all square. That meant extra holes, a prospect neither of us relished. Thankfully, it seemed that our misery would end early. On the first extra hole I hit the green in regulation. Shelly missed the green, chipped up, and made bogey. When I rolled my birdie putt to within eighteen inches, I thought it was all over. In fact, as I was walking up to the ball, Shelly started to concede the putt, but then said, "No, I can't give that to you. It's for everything. You have to tap it in." I walked up to this kick-in-short putt, but the stocking cap I had been wearing all day had gotten on my last nerve, so I decided to take it off before tapping in. I reached up and grabbed it, but then decided, "No, I'll just finish." With the stocking cap hanging off the side of my head, I nonchalantly swatted at the little putt and promptly missed it. Out loud I said, "Oh, my God, I've missed it." I couldn't believe it. Shelly then birdied the second extra hole to win the match and the California Women's Amateur.

Now, in Augusta no less, I'd missed another short putt—not eighteen inches short, but short enough. For the second time in six months, I'd had a match firmly in my grasp, only to let my opponent hang around. It was stupid when it happened at Pebble Beach, and as I walked to the seventeenth tee at Augusta Country Club, it was stupid again.

Hollis and I both made good pars on seventeen, which meant everything came down to the last hole. All I had to do was halve the eighteenth hole. Once again, I reached the green in regulation, and once again, it looked as though the match was over. Then, in front of my father, the media, and a fairly large gallery, I three-putted again for bogey to lose the hole. At the end of regulation, the match was all square.

I could almost feel that stocking cap on my head. It was like reliving a nightmare. I had no business plodding through a play-off. I should have closed the match out on sixteen or seventeen, and when that didn't happen, I certainly should have won it on eighteen. I had never factored a play-off into the equation. As Hollis and I headed back to the first tee, I was enraged.

Compared to the last three holes, our one-hole play-off was anticlimactic. We both hit approach shots into the greenside bunker, and after I blasted out to twelve feet, Hollis hit her sand shot to within inches of the hole. My putt for par never had a chance. Hollis made par to win the match. She went on to win the tournament the next day, making her the only player ever to win three consecutive U.S. Junior Girls—another record.

After the match, I buried my head in my father's chest and wept for half an hour. He was wonderful. We talked about the match, and he consoled me. Then he said, "Why don't we go out and get a nice dinner, then go back to the hotel?"

Through sobs I said, "No, I think I want to hit some golf balls. I just need to hit balls to clear my head."

Father nodded and smiled, and the two of us trotted off to the range armed with a bushel of practice balls. With tears dripping onto my grips, my dad and I stood out on the range after everyone else had left the course, and I hit balls until the blisters on my hands ruptured and blood began to ooze from worn calluses. We worked on tempo and a few swing keys, and I can still hear Father's consoling voice as I hit shot after shot that afternoon. I couldn't take back the mistakes I'd made in Augusta, but I could learn from them. I stayed on that range with my dad until I purged all the bad swings I'd made coming down the stretch and cried away the negative thoughts that had crept into my skull.

Through sobs I said, "No, I think I want to hit some golf balls. I just need to hit balls to clear my head."

Father stayed with me until dark. Afterward we went out to dinner and crashed in our hotel. I was disappointed and completely spent, but I had to put it behind me. The U.S. Women's Amateur was just two days away.

✦ ✦ ✦

If there is a lonelier stretch of highway in America than Interstate 20 between Augusta and Atlanta, I don't want to see it. About seventy-five miles into our trip west along that lonesome road, the water pump in Father's car cratered, and we were stuck in the middle of nowhere. It couldn't have been more than twenty or thirty minutes before someone came along to help us, but it seemed like hours. After some good-ole-boy negotiating and a trip to the pine trees (we were miles from the nearest bathroom), Father got us back on our way. We arrived in Marietta, a northern suburb of Atlanta, just in time to check into a Holiday Inn and feast on yet another prime rib dinner before our busy week at Atlanta Country Club.

I remember being surprised how hilly the golf course was. Coming from California, I had seen plenty of hills, and I had played my share of sloping golf courses. In Atlanta, I assumed the terrain would be much like what we'd played in Augusta. It wasn't, to my advantage. I knew how to play uphill, downhill, and sidehill lies, and at Atlanta Country Club, which hosted a PGA Tour event for over twenty years, you were going to catch some unusual lies during a week of play. The greens, on the other hand, were relatively flat, which also worked to my advantage. With my aggressive putting style, I could feel comfortable rapping my putts at the hole once I got the right line. All things considered, I was happy with the venue.

Advancing to the match-play rounds seemed easy enough, but my matches were anything but a cakewalk. Carol Thompson, a great amateur who would play the Curtis Cup for many years, put up a strong fight in the opening match, but I beat her two-and-one in a thirty-six-hole match. Afterward, Father and I went back to the hotel where we swam, ate steaks, laughed, and shared a lot of father-and-daughter fun.

In the semifinals the next morning, I played one of the toughest and most memorable matches of my life against Lancy Smith. We were all square after a hard-fought thirty-six holes, and it was off to extra holes—again. The first hole at Atlanta Country Club is an uphill par-four with a green protected by bunkers in the front and on the left. After a good drive, I was so pumped up that I flew the green with my approach shot, while Lancy hit her approach onto the green, leaving herself an uphill eighteen-footer for birdie.

My chip from the back of the green was fast and hard, and although I hit it well, the ball rolled ten feet past the hole. At that moment I had to fight the thoughts of my loss to Hollis the week before. This was a different golf course under different circumstances, and I was not going to let any negativity sneak into my brain at this critical juncture. I calmly watched as Lancy lagged her birdie putt to within tap-in range. I conceded her par, and then stood over the ten-footer I had left to halve the hole and continue the match. My putting had been good all year; I was an aggressive putter; I knew the line. It was just a matter of going through my routine and making a good stroke.

When the putt hit the back of the hole and went in, I heard a shout from the hillside adjacent to the green. *"Hey, hey!"* When I turned, I saw my dad pumping his fist in the air. Tears welled up in my eyes, and I had to shake my head to regain my focus. There was still golf left, but at that moment I knew I was going to win the match.

Lancy played well. We both made pars on the par-five second hole and then, on the par-three third (our thirty-ninth hole of the day), I hit my tee shot in the front bunker and Lancy hit hers in the back bunker. Once again I had to fight the thoughts of my play-off with Hollis, when we both hit our tee shots into the bunker. Lancy was the first to play this time, and when she hit a marginal bunker shot and left herself a difficult downhill putt for par, I relaxed and hit my bunker shot to within three feet. She missed, I made, and without even realizing it, I had played myself into the finals of the U.S. Women's Amateur.

After the thirty-nine-hole slugfest with Lancy, my final match with Beth Berry was almost anticlimactic, even though it went down to the last hole. With a par on our thirty-fifth hole of the day, I brought the match dormie, which meant I was one-up with one hole to play. The eighteenth at Atlanta Country Club is a dogleg left par-five, with water on the left side of the fairway that extends in front of the green. After laying up in front of the water with my second shot, I played a conservative third shot to the center of the green while Beth was in the process of making a routine par. This should have been it. All I had to do was two-putt and I would win the match and the championship, but as I knew all too well, that isn't as easy as it sounds.

I made a good birdie putt that died eighteen inches above the hole, and all at once the memories of that afternoon at Pebble Beach came flooding back. I studied that eighteen-inch putt from every conceivable angle, and I concentrated on it like no other putt. Beth must have said "That's good" three or four times and I didn't even hear her. There was no way I was going to repeat the mistakes I had made in the California Woman's Amateur or the U.S. Junior Girls. This time I was going to make it. Finally, Beth walked over and picked up my ball mark. She extended her hand, and for a moment I didn't understand what had happened. Then I heard the applause, and the cheers, and I realized that I had just won the U.S. Women's Amateur as a sixteen-year-old, becoming the youngest woman in history to capture that title—a record that still stands almost thirty years later.

By the time Father and I got back to the Holiday Inn, the hotel staff had put "Congratulations, Laura Baugh" on their roadside marquee. That was the first indication that people outside the confines of the tournament gallery actually noticed I'd won. Perhaps I was naive, but nothing could have prepared me for the media circus that followed.

The *Los Angeles Times* devoted a quarter-page to my photo and another twenty column inches to the story of my victory, an unheard-of amount of coverage for women's amateur golf at that time. I didn't look like a lot of the other golfers and I didn't dress like other golfers either. My little red sleeveless tennis dress captured the attention of the print and television reporters. It was so different from anything any other golfer wore at that time.

The media attention didn't stop with my dresses, nor did it end the week after my victory. From the time of my National Pee Wee victories, I had received a lot of media attention, so getting calls from reporters was not unusual. But I wasn't prepared for the flood of requests that came after my U.S. Amateur victory. My mom and I still didn't have a phone in our Olive apartment, so when a Los Angeles television station wanted me to appear on one of the local talk shows, they had to call my school to find me. When Disney wanted me to play a cameo role in the movie *The Love Bug II, Herbie Rides Again*, they had to contact my dad. I even appeared on the *Lawrence Welk Show*, ballroom dancing with the great band leader in a homemade dress my mother had sewn together, but only after producers had tracked me down through their network's Los Angeles affiliate.

Later that year I was named *Golf Digest*'s Most Beautiful Golfer, and within weeks of that honor, I was named the *Los Angeles Times*'s Woman of the Year, an incredible honor and one I didn't fully appreciate at the time. Even when the paper held an invitation-only reception for me aboard the *Queen Mary*, I was more excited about seeing my brother

Beau (who had come out to California to go to Cal State Long Beach) than any of the dignified hoopla the *Times* had orchestrated. In fact, after shaking hands and thanking everyone in the receiving line, Beau and I slipped below deck and played around in the unfilled swimming pool while the adults continued to drink and chat and socialize.

Several months later, long after my fifteen minutes of fame should have expired, I was invited to play in the Suzuki Invitational, an LPGA Tour event in Los Angeles. Early in that tournament, I had a hole-in-one on one of the par-threes and, as a result, I won a motorcycle. It wasn't a new motorcycle, however. The USGA had strict guidelines on what amateurs could and could not accept without violating the rules of amateur status, so one of the local police officers drove it around the parking lot a few times to ensure it was technically a "used" vehicle. At seventeen years old, I had no interest in riding a motorcycle, especially in my neighborhood, so I moved the bike into our apartment and it became a permanent stool for our kitchenette bar.

I became a sort of celebrity at Woodrow Wilson High School, elected Homecoming Princess by the student body my junior year even though I had very few close friends in school, and never, ever, not-in-a-million-years would I have invited friends over to my apartment. Because of my grades I was in an experimental college program similar to the advanced placement programs offered in high schools today, which limited my contact with other students my own age. Six of us attended Cal State Long Beach classes on the second floor of Woodrow Wilson High School, and the only classes where we mingled with other students at our grade level was physical education.

Because of that college program, coupled with the attention I received from the media, I was faced with one of the most difficult choices of my life. Late in 1972, a counselor from Stanford University, the school I had always dreamed of attending, asked if he could visit my mother and me in our Olive apartment. There was no way I would allow anyone from Stanford to come to Olive. From the time I was old enough to start thinking about college, the only school for me had been Stanford. First I wanted to follow in my father's footsteps and go to law school. Father convinced me that lawyers spent more time in the library than in the courtroom, so I changed my mind and decided I wanted to go to dental school. All my career aspirations included Stanford, though. To have a representative from that school calling sent goose bumps up my arms.

I became a sort of celebrity at Woodrow Wilson High School, elected Homecoming Princess by the student body my junior year even though I had very few close friends in school.

We met him in my grandparents' apartment, and within minutes I was offered an academic scholarship to Stanford. After the initial shock wore off, I replayed the conversation in my mind and realized that, not only was I being offered financial assistance, I was offered a four-year academic free ride to the school of my dreams. Stunned and ecstatic, I fought the temptation to accept the offer on the spot. After all, this was a life-changing decision and I didn't want to rush into something this major without thinking things through. I thanked the counselor and told him I would be in touch. One of the things I needed to consider was the effect Stanford would have on my golf game. Like many schools in that pre–Title IX era,

Stanford did not have a women's golf team, so my golf game would take a long hiatus. Even though my tuition would be covered, I would have to get a job in order to live, and a job would completely eliminate golf from my college agenda. I had played the game every day of my life since I was two years old; giving it up for four years was something I had to ponder long and hard.

Within weeks of that meeting with the Stanford counselor, my dilemma intensified. Earlier in the year, as part of the media frenzy surrounding my amateur victory, I played in an exhibition pro-am with Arnold Palmer and Dave Marr. It was the first time I had met Arnold, and he was the perfect gentleman. Later I learned he was equally impressed with me, or at least impressed enough that he mentioned me to his longtime agent Mark McCormack, founder of the International Management Group. That wasn't the first time McCormack had heard my name. Frank Hannigan, then assistant executive director of the USGA, told McCormack that he needed to sign me as an IMG client, so McCormack decided to give me a call.

Our first official meeting took place at the famed Los Angeles Country Club. I was a seventeen-year-old high school girl trying to decide whether or not to give up golf and accept a scholarship to Stanford, and I was playing golf with the most powerful sports agent in the world and John DeLorean, the now infamous former chairman of Pontiac. It didn't take long for Mark to get down to business. He told me that even though I wasn't eligible to join the LPGA Tour until after my eighteenth birthday, I could travel to Japan, work on my game, and make a healthy income from endorsements before earning my tour card.

My quandary was clear. If I chose to turn professional, which would mean a guaranteed income greater than anything I dreamed possible at that time, I would have to turn down the scholarship to Stanford. If I accepted the scholarship to Stanford, I could kiss my golf career good-bye. I was talented, but nobody could go a minimum of four years (more like eight, if I followed through with my dental school dreams) without hitting a golf ball, then pick the game back up and compete at the highest level. My choice was simple: Stanford or golf, education or career; I couldn't have both.

In the end, my decision came down to timing. I figured that if I turned pro at age seventeen, I could play golf for ten years and still be only twenty-seven years old—young enough to go back to school, start a family, and structure a second career. Although my mom and dad both gave me advice, the decision was mine, and I made it. I told my father to work out the details with Mr. McCormack, which he did in the dining room of Arnold Palmer's Bay Hill Club in Orlando, December 1972.

Before the falling of the giant ball in Times Square ushered in 1973, and four months before my eighteenth birthday, my first official act as a professional golfer was to borrow my grandmother's phone. I called the nice college counselor, thanked him for his interest, then politely turned down a full academic scholarship to Stanford University.

Within a month, I was on board an airplane bound for Tokyo.

CHAPTER 4

FAR EASTERN CELEBRITY

ROLEX GUARANTEED ME A THOUSAND dollars for my first trip to Japan, a virtual fortune to a seventeen-year-old from the Olive section of Long Beach. All I had to do was show up, wear a green and gold outfit (the official Rolex colors), play in two golf tournaments, and mingle with various Japanese executives and members of the press. What could be easier? Fly overseas, smile, wave, play golf, and get paid. I could do it with my eyes closed. Like most things in life, though, the trip turned out to be quite a bit different from what I had envisioned.

First, I didn't own any green and gold outfits, and since I wouldn't actually get a check until I showed up in Tokyo, Mom and I had to be creative in assembling my wardrobe. Armed with some money Rolex had advanced and a couple of color swatches, we trotted off to the local fabric warehouse and bought enough matching green and gold material so Mom could cut and stitch some pieces together. The end result was a series of dresses that Rolex and the other Japanese sponsors loved. No one knew they were homemade, and as far as I could tell, no one cared.

Nor did anyone know that this fresh, new professional golfer was flying from Los Angeles to Tokyo without enough money in her pocket to buy a ham and cheese sandwich at the airport. We were, for lack of a better word, poor. Mom, who by the time I turned pro had been divorced from Father for four years, had never worked outside the home, and she stored alimony and child support in classic depression-survivor fashion. Of course we ate, and we had clothes and transportation, and I had the opportunity to play golf around the world (which was remarkable given our economic circumstances), but there were never any extras. I didn't think twice about flying standby with absolutely no cash, so that's what I did. Once I arrived at the various tournament sites, private housing was always available, and since I wasn't old enough to rent cars, someone from the club was always at the airport holding a little sign with my name on it. Host families fed me, drove me where I needed to go, and generally supported me while I was playing golf in their towns, so never having money had become routine. This trip was no exception. Even though I was wearing a brand-new Rolex and a corporate-colored dress, the fact that I was flying halfway around the world without enough money to tip a bellman was not a big deal to me.

I had done it plenty of times before, such as when I had qualified for the Curtis Cup team. That time, I traveled to England and spent a month playing the matches, as well as competing in the Women's British Amateur and playing numerous exhibitions at St. Andrews and other places throughout the United Kingdom. I never knew who picked up the tab for that trip, but I always assumed it was the USGA, the R&A, or a combination of the two. Then when I was seventeen, I traveled to Buenos Aires as a member of the World Cup Team. Jane Booth, Martha Caraway, and I represented the United States and we won the World Cup handily. Once again, I assumed that the USGA took care of my expenses, meager as they were.

Both those trips gave me a sense of what it was like to travel abroad on a budget, but Argentina taught me a number of other important lessons as well. When we first arrived in South America, I thought I would be the coolest player on the team since I spoke Spanish. That was my first mistake. Within minutes of landing in Buenos Aires, I realized that the language I had learned in Southern California wasn't even close to that spoken by Argentineans. After hailing a cab, I rattled off a destination in what I thought was fluent Spanish, but the answer I got from the cabbie might as well have been in Swahili. The Southern California/Mexican version of Spanish I had picked up wasn't exactly the same as the Argentinean version. Whatever I said must have been misinterpreted as "Drive as fast and as recklessly as humanly possible," because that's exactly what every driver did. More than once, it seemed inevitable that I was going to become a South American traffic statistic, and Mom would to have to borrow money from Father to fly my body back to Long Beach.

Luckily, we survived the bat-out-of-hell cabbies and otherwise had a wonderful trip. After defeating Great Britain in the finals, we prepared to return to the United States as World Cup champions. The women's finals had concluded one day before the men's finals, and rather than stick around to watch Ben Crenshaw and the rest of the American team, we were supposed to fly back to the States the morning after our victory. Although disappointed we couldn't cheer on the men, we were all pretty happy to be going home. After we piddled around with luggage and shared overzealous good-byes with everyone we'd met, Martha, Jane, and I checked out of our hotel right on time to make our flight. Then, as we were riding to Mazazo International Airport, laughing and joking and recalling our World Cup victory, a bomb exploded on the twenty-third floor of the hotel, killing and wounding dozens of innocent people.

Fortunately, most of the men's team had left the hotel a few hours earlier to go to the golf course, but Ben Crenshaw and Vinny Giles were still in their rooms on the fifth floor when the blast occurred. No competitors were injured in the blast, but the impact of the explosion hit us all. I'd seen bombings and hijackings on television, but nothing like this. Hotel bombings didn't happen in 1972, or at least in my seventeen-year-old world they didn't. Later that summer, as terrorists kidnapped and killed a group of Israeli athletes at the Munich Olympic Games, the whole world woke up to the realization that it did happen, and it could happen to anyone. None of us left Buenos Aires unaffected, and the bombing stuck with each of us for a long time afterward. We had awakened to the realization that, while most people thought of us as athletes, there were some people in the world who thought of us as targets.

As I now sat on the plane headed for Japan, fastening the seat belt around my Rolex-green dress and bringing my seat back and tray table to their upright and locked positions, the Buenos Aires incident came flooding back into my mind. I said a little prayer of thanks for everything I had. Granted, I didn't have a lot of material things, growing up alone with Mom in California, but nobody had ever blown up a hotel in Los Angeles, and no terrorists had ever killed anyone in Olive. We didn't have a lot, but in retrospect, we had everything. I had been fortunate to play golf at the highest amateur levels and win, and now I was embarking on a career as a professional athlete. I had an agent, an endorsement deal, and a life that most people in the world wouldn't dream possible. "God bless America," I said to myself as the wheels of the airplane touched the Tokyo asphalt. I was truly lucky.

A representative from IMG's Tokyo office was to meet me at the airport, and I hoped he would recognize me so I wouldn't have to wait alone at the gate. I'd never been to Asia, and while the trip excited me, I didn't like the idea of being alone that far away from home. Unlike the other places I'd visited, it was impossible for a blonde American girl to blend into a crowd in Tokyo.

> *"God bless America," I said to myself as the wheels of the airplane touched the Tokyo asphalt.*

As the jet taxied toward the gate, I realized we wouldn't be exiting directly into the terminal. Metal stairs were being rolled up beside us on the tarmac, which meant we would unload outside and work our way through the airport to retrieve our baggage. That was a little distressing, especially since I had never met the person who was picking me up. Making matters worse, a gaggle of photographers clamored around the bottom of the stairs. Obviously, a dignitary or rock star or some other major celebrity was on the flight with me, and the entire Tokyo press corps had turned out to cover his arrival. I hoped I didn't get lost in the crowd.

It took a few minutes to sink in. As I got off the plane things started bustling below me, and I got the distinct impression the photographers were looking at me. But that couldn't be right, could it? For a brief instant I understood how the Beatles must have felt when they first arrived in New York. Paul McCartney said that when the band exited the airplane at LaGuardia, a huge crowd starting cheering and screaming, and Paul, John, George, and Ringo assumed that the president must be nearby. They looked over their shoulders to see if there was another plane behind them before realizing that the cheers were for them. As I started down the stairs, cameras flashed and photographers crowded the bottom of the ramp. I instinctively glanced back to see if I was in someone else's shot, but with no one coming off the plane behind me, it slowly dawned on me that these people were photographing me.

"What's going on?" I asked the IMG representative who introduced himself at the bottom of the stairs.

"You're already a celebrity," he said.

I might have laughed out loud, I don't remember. I certainly didn't believe him, just like I didn't expect that kind of reception at the airport. Nor could I have imagined what awaited me at the hotel, the golf course, and virtually everywhere I traveled in Tokyo. Masses of people flocked around me, waiting in lobbies and standing in lines at the golf course. I was shocked. It wasn't as though I was a professional superstar. I had yet to play one round of golf as a professional. But the Japanese people treated me as though I had won every major championship on every continent and then saved Tokyo from Godzilla in my spare time.

The overwhelming welcome was more than flattering, but I didn't get it. Right after I arrived, IMG scheduled a press conference. When we arrived, the room was packed. I stayed for over two hours answering questions and posing for photographs. Then I went to the golf course where a sea of fans lined up to watch me walk around, hit a few balls, and roll a couple of putts. By that time I'd grown accustomed to galleries, but the sheer number of people who came out to see me was staggering. I couldn't focus on my practice. I was too busy staring with my jaw agape as more and more people swarmed around me to watch.

It surprised me how such a large crowd could be so courteous. Japanese manners are astonishing, but I loved their enthusiasm the most. The gallery knew golf and appreciated everything I did in the game. I responded with lots of smiles and waves. I shook hands, signed autographs, and interacted with as many fans as possible, given the size of the crowds. I couldn't get over how well I was being received, even though I didn't win either of the golf tournaments. Each day the crowds grew larger, and the cheers grew louder.

At the conclusion of the trip, I graciously thanked everyone in Japan for the overwhelming hospitality, then I returned home to begin preparations for the LPGA Tour's qualifying school. Little did I know how my brief trip would snowball into one of the most lucrative and rewarding relationships of my career. Not long after I returned home, IMG came to me with an idea that, at the time, was so unique I thought they had to be kidding. According to Mark McCormack, the people at Japan's version of *Golf Digest* wanted me to pose for a calendar. Of course, my first thoughts were the pin-up girls—Marilyn Monroe, Jayne Mansfield, and, in my day, Raquel Welch. I wasn't so sure that was the kind of thing I should be doing. *Sports Illustrated* hadn't considered a swimsuit calendar at that time, and Cindy Crawford was in kindergarten, so the concept of a sports calendar didn't connect with me at first. *Playboy* was the only magazine I knew that published a calendar, and I certainly wasn't interested in that. I was a golfer. Why on earth would anyone want a calendar of me? My next thought went straight into the gutter. I assumed these folks expected me to disrobe for some of the photos, something I was not about to discuss.

The rest of the guys at IMG bent over backwards to assure me that nudity had never come up in the discussions, and no one expected me to do anything untoward or uncomfortable. These people were golfers, and this was going to be a golf calendar. Today that's a concept that everyone can understand and readily accept, but at the time of these discussions, no one knew what a golf calendar was—including me. And no one knew what the market was for a glossy calendar with twelve photos of a young girl in various golf poses. I, for one, was skeptical, but I also knew that Mark McCormack and IMG had been on the forefront of marketing athletes for over fifteen years, and if they thought it was worth a try, who was I to question it? After all, it was flattering to think that somebody might actually pay to have photos of me hanging in their offices or living rooms for a whole year. I still wasn't sure the idea would work, but I agreed to give it a shot if I could be assured there wouldn't be any lurid or suggestive photos in the calendar. If we chose to take some bathing-suit shots (which I thought was fine, especially for the summer months), the poses would be tasteful. I wanted the final OK. *Golf Digest* didn't have a problem with that and so, in short order, I became golf's first calendar girl.

They turned out to be the hottest-selling calendars in Japan. So popular, in fact, that I posed for new calendars every year for thirteen years. People actually queued up for over two hours outside stores to buy them, and most vendors sold out as fast as they could get them. It never ceased to amaze me how people in Japan responded, even after I'd been doing the calendars for more than ten years. The 1987 calendar sold just as well as the 1977 calendar. Even so, after I hit my thirties, I decided to retire from the calendar business before anyone at *Golf Digest* told me it was time to quit. By that time, golf, swimsuit, and all sorts of other calendars had become hot sellers worldwide. I was the first, but after we wrapped the shoot for the thirteenth annual edition of the Laura Baugh Calendar, the market had become saturated and highly competitive. I was a mom by then, and I wasn't the least bit interested in trying to look twenty-two years old. If I was going to get out, I wanted to do it on my own terms while the product was still popular.

There were other things to do. Because of my popularity in Japan, I had my own weekly television show that aired over the Tokyo Broadcast System. By American standards it was pretty silly. I played golf and chatted with various Japanese celebrities, many of whom couldn't speak a word of English. I never learned much Japanese either, so the conversations were often stilted, and the quality of the golf varied. At times the players were quite good and very competitive, but on other occasions the skill level bordered on mediocre. During one episode I was supposed to play with the country's premier sumo wrestler. He knew less about golf than I did about wrestling. After five whiffs on the first tee, the big guy finally made contact, after which I was supposed to say, "Good shot!" I'm not sure how well that translated to a Japanese audience, but it was roll-on-the-ground funny here in the states.

Equally funny was a series of advertisements that Arnold Palmer and I did together that aired in Japan. Because our respective sportswear lines were marketed together, Japanese agencies often packaged Arnold and me as a couple in their television ads. In some we even had kids by our sides, all nicely dressed in Arnold Palmer and Laura Baugh sportswear. I guess we looked like the perfect American family, even though Arnold (about twenty-five years my senior) said, "I'm not sure they'll accept me as Laura's husband." The commercials were pretty strange. Filmed in the Vasquez Rocks, a remote desert area a couple of hours outside Los Angeles, they cast Arnold, the kids, and me as a pioneer family in the Old West. In one ad we all danced around a campfire along with several cowboys and Indians, the family wearing golf attire, while the cowboys had six-guns strapped to their hips and the Indians wore face paint and full-feathered headdresses. Another ad had Arnold and me riding in a stagecoach that was being robbed. A masked bandit rode his horse up to our charging coach, and after he forced it to stop, the stagecoach door swung open and, voilà, Arnold and I leaned out holding a birthday cake. "Happy birthday, America," Arnold said, while I was waving and smiling at the camera.

After several hours of shooting that one, Arnold turned to me and said, "Laura, can you believe we're doing this?"

"No, not really," I said.

Then, looking more rugged than any of our cowboy actors, Arnold tilted his head, put his hands on his hips, and said, "Good. Let's go play golf."

"Play golf!" I said. I was hot, tired, and the desert dirt that hadn't blown into my mouth had settled under my hairline. The last thing I wanted to do was play golf, but you couldn't say no to Arnold. Off we went to the golf course.

I did other Japanese television ads for soft drinks, salad dressing, watches, and motorcycles, but none quite as bizarre as the ones with Arnold. There were magazine interviews and talk shows, and I even recorded two Japanese songs that sold remarkably well. Mark McCormack would later tell me that my photo had, at one point or another, been on the cover of every single national magazine in Japan. That in itself was mind-boggling. I never won a single tournament over there, but, along with Arnold Palmer, I became one of the most recognized American celebrities in the country.

A masked bandit rode his horse up to our charging coach, and after he forced it to stop, the stagecoach door swung open and, voilà, Arnold and I leaned out holding a birthday cake.

There were some drawbacks, but not many. After a while I carried black wigs when I traveled in Japan so I could walk around without being recognized. I never felt threatened in any way, but I did get a taste of what celebrity life is like. I couldn't go to a gym or a restaurant, or go window shopping on the streets of Tokyo, without being recognized and mobbed by large groups of very polite but very persistent autograph seekers. Hotel stairwells soon served as my workout venues, and I became a room-service connoisseur whenever I visited the country. It was a small price to pay, though. I loved the Japanese experience and the Japanese people. What started out as a one-thousand-dollar corporate outing continued to grow and evolve into a bond with the people that has lasted my entire adult life. Even after the advertising campaigns, the calendar sales, and the television shows stopped, my relationship with the Japanese people remained intact. It's been a decade since I last posed for a golf calendar, but I am still a well-known figure in the country. Believe it or not, I was asked to do another Laura Baugh golf calendar at the age of forty-four!

Who would have ever thought it possible? But it's still in the works for the millennium.

✦ ✦ ✦

In the spring of 1973, after I returned home from my first trip to Japan, there were a lot of other things on my mind. Because of the organization's rules, I couldn't join the LPGA Tour until after my eighteenth birthday in May, but even then I wasn't immediately guaranteed a tour card as a birthday present. Like everyone else who wanted to play the LPGA Tour, I had to go through qualifying school, which wasn't a school at all but a tournament to determine who could play competitively on the LPGA Tour. I was under a tremendous amount of personal pressure to earn my card. IMG had already negotiated a lucrative endorsement deal with the Wilson Sporting Goods company, and I was already wearing the Wilson logo and carrying Wilson equipment as my contract stipulated. If I didn't qualify to play the LPGA Tour, my endorsement value to Wilson would drop through the floor. At that time there were no minitours like there are today, and Europe and Asia still had very few events for women. So a female golfer either played the LPGA, or, for the most part, stayed home.

A month shy of eighteen I'm hitting some range balls at Mission Hills, where I was doing some promotional work for the LPGA Tour's Colgate Dinah Shore Classic. I played in my first tournament as a pro about a month later. (AP/WIDE WORLD PHOTOS)

I was not going to stay home.

The LPGA Tour held its qualifying school in June at the Indian Hills Country Club in Marietta, Georgia, where I had won the U.S. Amateur championship. Obviously, I had great memories of the town, so I entered Q-School with a lot of confidence. The golf course also suited my game. Narrow fairways were lined with enough out-of-bounds stakes to build a new clubhouse, and the greens were well protected, meaning anyone who could hit the ball straight would do well there. Accuracy was the strongest part of my game. I was a little nervous, but I was also very confident. I had won most junior events I'd entered and there was no reason, in my mind, that I shouldn't pick right up and win most events I played as a professional, starting with Q-School.

The qualifying criterion was much different in those days from what it is now. Back in 1973 the Q-School tournament wasn't really a tournament in the sense that a certain number of winners earned their cards and advanced to the tour; it was more of a playing-ability test. All you had to do was average 78 or better for four rounds. If one hundred girls averaged 78, then the tour would issue one hundred cards. If no one averaged 78, no cards would be issued. The tour wanted to grow, but they also wanted to maintain a certain quality level. The general consensus was that if you couldn't break 79, you didn't have any business playing professional golf on the LPGA Tour. But if you could break 79, it was come one, come all.

I couldn't envision having trouble with the target score, but I also couldn't have imagined the temperature would be fifty degrees in June and that rain would fall for four straight days in Atlanta. From the time we teed off on

Thursday until the final putt fell on Sunday, the weather ranged from a moderate sprinkle to a major downpour with temperatures never edging above sixty. It was miserable. Under those conditions, nothing was a sure bet.

To make matters worse, when I arrived at the club I learned that in order to play in the Q-School tournament, each player had to pass a written multiple-choice test on the rules of golf. "You're kidding," I said to an LPGA official. When she politely informed me that no indeed, they weren't kidding, I pleaded, "I didn't know anything about a test. I didn't prepare for a test!" Communication was never one of the LPGA's strongest suits in those days, and most girls had found out about the rules exam via the grapevine. I knew I hadn't read anything about it in what few materials I'd received, and I tried to make that point to the tournament officials in Atlanta. My cries fell on deaf ears, however, and like everyone else who participated in the qualifying tournament, I had to take a written rules exam the Wednesday evening before play was to begin.

You couldn't tee off in the tournament unless you had passed the test, but you wouldn't find out if you had passed the test until right before you were to tee off in the tournament. It was nerve-wracking, to say the least. I showed up at the club early on Thursday morning, assuming that this would be like a college exam and the grades would be posted on a bulletin board. They weren't, and I was advised to go ahead and warm up for my round. "We'll inform you before you're scheduled to play," I was told.

"But I'm scheduled to play in an hour," I said.

"Then you'll learn whether or not you've passed in less than an hour," came the response.

Wet, cold, and disheveled, I marched off to the practice tee where I tried to prepare myself for the most important tournament of my newfound professional career, even though I wasn't sure I would even be allowed to play. What would I tell the people at IMG? I was sure I'd done well on the test—the questions weren't that difficult—but I could rationalize anything, especially when presented with multiple options. "If a ball is within the confines of a lateral hazard, your drop options are: A; B; C; D; A and C; B and D; A, B, and C; none of the above; all of the above." But, what if you chose to play it rather than taking a drop? What then? Oh, God, what would I say to Mark McCormack? "Hey, Mark, thanks for all you've done for me, but I didn't get my tour card, not because I can't play, but because I'm an idiot." And how would he explain to the people at Wilson that their new star endorser wouldn't be playing the tour because she couldn't pass a rules test? Oh, God, what would I tell my family?

By the time the starter called me to the first tee, I was a basket case. "Did I pass? Did I?" I asked.

The starter, a volunteer member of Indian Hills, had no idea what I was babbling about, so he quietly motioned to an LPGA official.

"Did I pass? Can I play?" I asked in rapid succession. These people needed to answer me and they needed to answer right then and there.

"Let's see," the official said, painstakingly checking his list.

Come on. Come on, I mentally pleaded. *Can I play or not? Turn the page, check your list, and tell me if my professional career is over before it starts, or if I actually get a chance to show you what I can do. Come on!*

"Yes, there it is," he finally said. "You passed. Good luck and play well."

I proceeded to hit the worst snap-hook of my life off that first tee, and I opened the tournament with a double bogey. Soon I settled into a rhythm, and while my scores weren't great, they were certainly lower than the 78 average the LPGA had set as its benchmark. After fifty-four holes it looked as though three of us—Mary Bea Porter, Barbara Bodie, and I—would earn our cards. A lot of other good players wouldn't, including Jan Stephenson, who had already made a splash in Australia. Jan wouldn't gain her card until 1974, and she would go on to be named Rookie of the Year then. But in 1973, the brutal weather in Atlanta got to her.

It also got to the three of us who eventually qualified. During the final nine holes, we suffered through so many rain delays, I didn't think we would finish. As Barbara, Mary, and I were standing in the maintenance building during the final delay, all of us had resigned ourselves to coming back out on Monday to finish the last few holes. Then the superintendent and tournament director pulled into the maintenance building and told us we were the only three players who had a chance to earn our cards, so even though the course was virtually unplayable, if we wanted to finish, we could.

All of us agreed to play in the downpour, and all of us qualified easily. I finished bogey, bogey, bogey to earn my card, and Mary Bea finished bogey, par, bogey to earn medalist honors. As the three of us stood on the eighteenth tee looking like drowned mice, I did some quick calculating and determined that if I parred the last hole, I would break

300 for the four days. That meant I could make a 15 on the final hole and still earn my card. I couldn't help but smile as a great burden was lifted.

I was a full-fledged, card-carrying LPGA professional, and I was ready to take the world by storm.

CHAPTER *5*

Struggles

I PLAYED IN SIXTEEN LPGA Tour events in 1973 and made $14,657—a paltry sum by today's million-dollar standards, but good enough during the Nixon years that I finished in the top thirty-five on the money list and earned the Rookie of the Year title.

Coupled with the thousand dollars I had earned from my trip to Japan, my earnings rocketed me from the depths of a struggling existence in Olive to the comfortable strata of American middle class. Given my background, I could have easily lived on fifteen thousand dollars. I was only eighteen years old, and I had survived on far less for many years. Unlike those women on tour who struggled to get by, the next meal and tomorrow's caddie fees were never issues for me. From the beginning of my career, the basics—food, travel, living expenses, and savings for a rainy day—were covered. Everything else was gravy, and in those early years, there was plenty of gravy to go around.

Along with the Japanese contracts and the Wilson Sporting Goods deal, IMG did a magnificent job capitalizing on the fact that I was demonstrably different from any other professional on tour. I didn't look like them, and I didn't dress, speak, or behave like the other women in golf. I knew I was different and a certain, very real distance developed between us. No other tour player had grown up sneaking free rounds on public golf courses, and very few had lived the high-volume family drama that had permeated the Baugh household. I was a decade younger than the average tour professional, which made it more difficult for me to fit in.

The differences were evident my first week on tour when I showed up at the golf course wearing a backless cotton blouse. My plan had been to work on those pesky two-piece bathing suit tan lines while working on my long-iron shots, but somehow this was lost on most of my fellow professionals. Arriving on the first tee in a bikini couldn't have caused a bigger stir. "Did you see what she had on? What kind of shirt was that? Who does she think she is?" Later in the week I showed up without socks because I wanted to get some sun on my ankles. "Can't she afford socks? What is she trying to prove?"

If I had been a little older, I probably could have avoided the catty chatter, at least for my first week on tour. Fortunately, it didn't bother me, and it bothered corporate sponsors even less. Shortly after making my LPGA debut, I signed a deal to represent Rolex, and not long after that, I joined Johnny Miller and Lanny Wadkins as one of Ford Motor Company's "Young Thunderbirds," a clever marketing tie-in between young athletes and the company's sleek Thunderbird coupe. I'm not sure our posing in front of the newest model Thunderbird caused young people to flock to the showrooms, but I never questioned the logic of the campaign. As far as I was concerned, the Thunderbird deal was a godsend, not so such for the money but for the perks. Ford provided a Thunderbird in every city I visited, and as an eighteen-year-old who wasn't old enough to rent a car, a new vehicle at my disposal was a lifesaver. The company also gave me a Thunderbird to drive when I was home. We had squeezed the last mile out of the 1967 GTO that Mom and I had driven across the country after my parents' divorce, so a new car in the garage was like manna from heaven.

Having a garage wasn't bad either. About the same time I was picking out the color of my new Thunderbird, I signed an endorsement contract with the Hamlet, a golf course development in Delray Beach, Florida. Again, the money was modest by today's standards, but the real-estate developer understood the value of a tour player representing his property, so he gave me the use of a townhouse whenever I needed it. I also managed to sign another deal out west for a condominium in Palm Springs at the Canyon Resort.

My plan had been to work on those pesky two-piece bathing suit tan lines while working on my long-iron shots, but somehow this was lost on most of my fellow professionals.

I had gone from a one-bedroom flat in Olive, where the nightlife consisted of hookers on the street corners and domestic disturbances two doors down, to bicoastal golf-course residences complete with new cars, new clothes, a nice new Rolex, and more endorsement offers than I could handle. Before I knew it, David Crystal had approached me about designing my own line of women's golf clothing—an offer I accepted and a task I took very seriously—and television producers were constantly asking if I would make cameo appearances. Life had become a numbing swirl of offers, endorsements, and celebrity appearances. For a fee I would display your logo somewhere on my person, pose with your product, and star in your television and print ad campaign. For an even larger fee, I would come to your company golf outing, give a clinic, play golf with your best clients, and attend an after-round cocktail party where I would be as delightful and charming as you needed me to be. Then I would collect my check and head off to the next function at the next tournament in the next city.

I seemingly had it all, including the ultimate benchmark of iconoclastic celebrity: a stalker. (That situation quickly and quietly resolved itself when my mentally ill fan trotted onto the putting green at a Miami tour stop and introduced himself. After his arrest, things calmed down considerably.) Unfortunately, my life and my career were devoid of a number of other important things, not the least of which was a win on the LPGA Tour.

For twenty-five years I was known in the media as "Golf's Golden Girl," "Golf's Calendar Girl," "Golf's Consummate Mom," and finally "Golf's Tarnished Drunk." But in all that time, through all the hype, highs, lows, riches, and rags, I never won an LPGA Tour event. From age eighteen until my forty-third birthday, with only one year (when I was pregnant with my first child) completely away from the tour, I never once hoisted a trophy on the eighteenth green, never held the huge cardboard check that coat-and-tie-clad sponsors presented to the winner, never gave the winner's press conference, and never got the honor of playing the next year as a defending champion. The girl who had everything, who had won almost every tournament as a junior, and who still holds a spot in the record books as the youngest winner of the U.S. Women's Amateur, spent twenty-five winless years on the LPGA Tour.

There is no doubt I made a good living, both on and off the course, but as a competitor I knew that golf was about winning tournaments; and as my near-misses mounted and my winless streak continued into a second, third, fourth, then fifth and sixth season, the yoke around my neck became heavier each time I teed off. Certainly, there were times when I wondered if my life would have turned out differently if I had won a few tournaments, but I know now that the "what if" game gets you nowhere. The past, both good and bad, is beyond my control, and I refuse to ponder what might have been. As for the career disappointments, to quote the great Japanese professional Tommy Nakajima, "That's golf."

I know the problems in my personal life would have come my way in one form or another, whether I won fifty tournaments or never made a cut. I am an alcoholic with or without a victory, and the elements of my personality that led me down the darker paths of my life had nothing to do with winning, losing, or even playing golf. Not winning as a rookie—or as a second-year professional, or as a veteran, or as a seasoned veteran—was disappointing. But I made no excuses then, and I make no excuses now. One of the lessons I've learned as a recovering person is that golf is golf and life is life, and blurring the line between the two can be disastrous.

As a young woman who was expected to "take the LPGA by storm," I put a lot of pressure on myself to win, and when it didn't happen, I drove myself even harder. I had to win. I had given up Stanford for this career and, by God, I was going to make the most of it. I had been poor. I had been scoffed at, labeled "that Florida girl...you know, the one with the mother," and snubbed as an illegitimate intruder in the elite country club circles of my peers. But on the golf course, I knew what I could do. Not only was I legitimate, I was one of the best. On the golf course, I controlled my domain. No one could take away my accomplishments in the game, so after each near-miss I would bear down on myself, grinding harder and harder each time I teed off. Would this be the one? Could I finally break through this week? When would it come?

As weeks stretched into months, and months stretched into years without a victory, the pressures became frustrations, and the frustrations eventually gave way to anger. I'm not sure when self-doubt began to creep in, but when it did, I internalized all the years of near-misses and heartbreaking disappointments. I began to think some of my harshest critics might have been right. Maybe I had extended myself too far. Maybe I had let the endorsement money clutter my focus. Maybe my swing wouldn't hold up under tour pressure, or maybe I didn't have the right stuff to win at the highest competitive level. Maybe, maybe, maybe. At one point or another, all those doubts crept into my noggin.

I *could* have put all the doubt and pressure behind me in my first tournament as a professional. A week after slogging through the cold rain at Indian Hills Country Club, the Georgia sunshine came out and warm breezes dried out the course for the Lady Tara Classic, Atlanta's LPGA Tour event. I had just completed a four-round tournament at Indian Hills in miserable conditions, so I knew the golf course, and I had a lot of confidence in my ability to play it well. Just as it suited my game in Q-School, the golf course set up well for me in the drier, warmer conditions. I had the

Even a little soft shoe and body English couldn't help me with this short birdie putt that I missed at the 1973 Lady Tara Classic, my first tournament as a professional. I led the tournament for part of the weekend but eventually had to settle for second place behind Mary Mills. (CORBIS/BETTMAN-UPI)

advantage of a weeklong head start on the field. The other women had been in another city, playing another golf course, while I was focusing on every bump, hill, nook, and cranny of Indian Hills. My confidence was high, the weather was great, and after my backless blouse fashion faux pas, I nestled into the tournament as an early leader.

I led the Lady Tara by two shots in the early holes of the final round, and things seemed perfect. The pressure of Q-School was behind me, and my game had fallen into that elusive slot golfers call "the zone," where hundreds of components converge for a fleeting instant and the game seems so easy that you wonder why it took so long to figure it out. As I strolled around Indian Hills that sunny Sunday June afternoon, I knew that I was poised to win the first event I played as a newly anointed LPGA Tour professional.

Then Mary Mills, a tour veteran (fifteen years older than I) and former U.S. Open champion who had seven tour wins at that time, started creeping up the leader board with a few birdies. I didn't pay a great deal of attention. After one bogey early in the round, I nestled into the zone and reeled off a string of routine pars. The Lady Tara was my tournament to win. Middle of the fairways, middle of the greens, and this one was mine. When I reached seventeen, I had no idea how Mary was playing ahead of me, so I checked the scoreboard behind the seventeenth green. I was *too* focused. To my stunned amazement, I saw that Mary had not only caught me, she had passed me! Somewhere, somehow, Mary Mills had gone on a birdie barrage and jumped into the lead. I was one shot down with one and a half holes to play, facing a fifteen-foot birdie putt on the seventeenth. The tournament that had been mine to win was now mine to lose.

After taking a moment to collect myself, I said to my caddie, "Eighteen is playing tough. I better give this birdie a
run." He agreed. Mary was not likely to birdie eighteen, so if
I could make birdie at seventeen and par the eighteenth, I
would probably reclaim at least a share of the lead. I checked
my birdie putt from every conceivable angle, but I couldn't
stop my mind from wandering: How on earth had Mary
mounted such a huge charge in such a short time? I hadn't
heard any gallery roars, and I hadn't seen any unusual movement up ahead, but there she was, perched above me on the
leader board. A tournament that I was supposed to win…that
I seemed destined to win…was now slipping away.

I checked the line of my birdie putt on seventeen one
last time before going through my preshot routine. It
seemed easy enough. All I had to do was aggressively rap
the putt into the back of the hole, then par the eighteenth.
Victory was still within my grasp. I just had to grind my
way through two more holes in one under par.

When I hit the first putt, my heart sank. Adrenaline
rushed through my veins right in the middle of my stroke,
and what I intended to be an aggressive birdie effort turned
out to be a strong, definitive miss. I started saying, "Whoa,"
before the ball reached the hole. After it rolled six feet past, I
was visibly deflated. My best shot at catching Mary had just
roared past the hole, and now I was left with a six-footer for
par. "The zone" vanished. My confidence was shattered,
and the realization that I had probably let a victory slip
away slowly rolled into my brain. How could I have let it
happen? How could a win like that get away from me?

After going through a somewhat hurried preshot routine, I made what I thought was a good stroke, but my

six-foot par putt hit the edge of the hole and spun out. I had three-putted for bogey, handing the win to Mary on a silver platter.

After two-putting for par on the eighteenth and resigning myself to the fact that I had given the tournament away, I checked with the scorers to see exactly how Mary had made such a dramatic charge. What I learned shocked me even more. The scoreboard I had seen on the seventeenth was wrong. The reason I hadn't heard any uproarious crowd noise was because Mary *hadn't* jumped ahead of me. We were actually tied at that point, but the scoreboard operator on the seventeenth green had gotten it wrong. Unbeknownst to me, I was still sharing the lead and didn't need a birdie. All I needed was a two-putt par on the seventeenth and another par on the eighteenth and I would have tied Mary and been in a play-off. Certainly, I wouldn't have charged the birdie putt on seventeen. As it was, I had blown a tie for the lead because the scoreboard was wrong, and I thought Mary had taken a one-shot lead. Not only had I thrown it away, I had done so without cause. Mary won by one shot.

The loss cut deep, but I rationalized it by putting myself in a different mind-set. I was a professional now, and losses were going to happen. I had to put it behind me and prepare for the next week. Besides, finishing second in my first professional start wasn't that bad. A lot of women spent years on tour before breaking into the top five, and some veterans had gone several seasons without a top-ten finish. I had finished second right off the bat. The loss hurt, but I had to keep it in perspective. There were plenty of tournaments to come. I was only eighteen, and my whole professional life was ahead of me. I couldn't beat myself up too badly for

Me at age nine looking every bit the tomboy as I get ready to address a tee shot at Cocoa Rockledge in Florida. (COURTESY OF HALE BAUGH II)

It's a year later and now I'm ten years old but still in Cocoa Beach, although I'm not sure why I'm holding a wedge while on the practice green. Maybe I was practicing one of those old "stymie" shots. (COURTESY OF HALE BAUGH II)

My dad, Hale Sr., loved golf, and I know he was proud of my success. This was taken at Cocoa Beach in 1971 when I was sixteen, about two weeks before I won the U.S. Women's Amateur.
(COURTESY OF HALE BAUGH II)

This is one of my favorite posed shots of me without a golf club in my hand. The occasion is the 1974 Colgate-Dinah Shore Classic in Palm Springs, California. (AP/WIDE WORLD PHOTOS)

My brother Beau and I share a nice sibling moment, sometime in the mid-1970s. (LAURA BAUGH)

The outfit says it all—by the look on my face, I must have had a bad lie and was wondering which way the shot would go. In any event, it's 1978 and I was still looking for my first pro victory (and I still am).
(© LEONARD KAMSLER)

Arnold Palmer and I are dressed up in Old West regalia for a Japanese TV ad filmed in the 1970s. The commercial's premise had Arnold and me as husband and wife, even though we were about twenty-five years apart in age— but we did become good friends and remain so to this day.
(© TONY ROBERTS)

I'm not sure if I was even aware at the time of making a fashion statement, but I suppose this was one time you could have called me "the woman in black," the LPGA's counterpart to Gary Player on the men's side.

(© Leonard Kamsler)

Okay, if we're going to have me in black, why not white? It wasn't so much that I wanted to get noticed; I just wanted to look nice and look like a woman. After all, you don't see me in anything leopard skin, do you?

(© Tony Roberts)

My brothers Hale (dark suit) and Beau (white) join little sis at Christmas in 1987. (Laura Baugh)

I figured Chelsea had to put up with watching me beat practice balls, so I would occasionally give her a chance to show her stuff. This was in 1986, when she was about four years old. (© Leonard Kamsler)

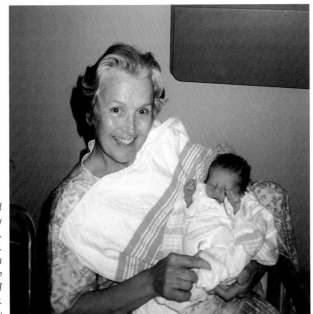

Mom holds one-day-old Robert Jess Cole, my fourth child of seven, born March 13, 1992. Mom and I have had a peculiar relationship over the years, but I will always love her. (LAURA BAUGH)

At the beach in a 1998 LPGA event, trying to find some more magic. (PETE FONTAINE PHOTO, © SportImages)

My oldest son, E. J., makes Mom feel right at home even at the practice range. (BY STEVE PRIEST)

blowing the Lady Tara. Victories would come someday soon. I was sure of it.

✦ ✦ ✦

Those victories never came. From 1974 through 1991 I finished second seven times and had twenty-two top-five finishes, but no LPGA Tour victories. In the process, I found some of the most imaginative and dramatic ways to finish second. In Chicago I birdied four of the last five holes to pull into a tie for the lead with Betty Burfeindt, only to watch as Betty sank an eight-foot birdie putt on the final hole to beat me by one. Then in Noblesville, Indiana, I shot a final-round 65 to gain a share of the lead with Judy Rankin and Hollis Stacy, only to lose to Hollis, my old U.S. Junior Girls nemesis, on the second hole of a sudden-death play-off. In Saint Paul, I missed a five-foot putt on the final hole to finish second, and in New Rochelle I closed with three straight birdies to finish one shot out of a play-off.

I couldn't beat myself up too badly for blowing the Lady Tara. Victories would come someday soon. I was sure of it.

Perhaps my biggest disappointment, however, came in California in March 1986. By that time I was living in La Quinta, a development right outside Palm Springs, and all my friends drove up to Costa Mesa to watch me play in the Uniden Invitational. After I shot 68-70-68, I held a four-shot lead going into the final eighteen, and friends I hadn't seen in years came out of the woodwork to cheer me on to victory. Even some of the guys who used to sneak out on Recreation Park Long Beach with me showed up in the gallery. Everyone thought this was going to be it. Finally, after thirteen years, I was going to break through with my first win on tour, and it was going to come near my home in front of people I'd known since high school. By the time the final threesome teed off on Sunday afternoon, a very partisan gallery had lined the first fairway shouting things like, "Come on, Laura, it's your time." I could almost feel the tension in the air as hundreds of people held their breath, hoping this would finally be it.

Mary Beth Zimmerman, who had won the week before in Phoenix, and Patty Sheehan, who also had a victory in the early part of 1986, both started the day four shots off my lead, and the three of us were paired together in the final group of the tournament. I was nervous, but I always had a few butterflies before teeing off. That was only natural. When I took out my three-iron on the tee of the par-five first hole, I could hear a nervous grumbling in the crowd, and I knew what was being said. "An iron on this hole? Boy, she is really playing it safe."

I was playing it safe but also smart. Since I couldn't reach the green with my second shot, it was more important for me to be in the fairway than it was to take a chance with a driver. Even if I boomed a tee shot into the fairway, I would have to lay up with my second shot, so the risk wasn't worth the reward. Mary Beth and Patty didn't think that way, though, and they both blasted tee shots well past my short-but-straight three-iron.

Unfortunately, my strategy didn't pay off. I three-putted the first green for bogey, and then proceeded to three-putt two more greens in the first nine holes. By all rights, I should have blown the lead, but neither Mary Beth nor Patty took advantage of my mishaps, and when I made birdies at ten and thirteen, I extended my lead back to four shots. A four-shot lead with five holes to play should have been plenty. All I had to do was par the last four holes and I would have my first win on tour, a win I desperately wanted.

By then I had my first daughter (Chelsea) and I had just finalized a divorce (my second). Life wasn't the basket of roses I had naively thought it would be when I first turned pro, or when I signed up for the calendars, or when I got married and began what I thought would be another phase of my life. But I was still young, financially secure, and still playing well enough to feel confident that I could win. After all, Ben Hogan played well but didn't become a legend until he was in his forties. Sam Snead won tour events in his fifties, and the timeless Kathy Whitworth proved that women could compete for decades. I was only thirty-one. My career was far from over. Now, with five holes to play on a golf course I knew well, in front of a crowd that wanted me to win almost as much I wanted it myself, my time had finally come.

Then, on fourteen, I drove the ball into the middle of the fairway and hit what I thought was a great approach shot. I made a good swing, and I caught the ball just the way I intended. When I looked up, however, the first words out of my mouth were, "Get down!" The ball took one hop, jumped beyond the flag, and stopped behind the green. I had hit it fifteen yards farther than I thought I could with that golf club. I had missed yet another green.

This time I was angry with myself. I hit a good shot, but I had let adrenaline get the best of me; now I was faced with another tricky up-and-down effort. After taking my time and examining the shot, I hit my chip beyond the flag and proceeded to miss the comeback putt for par. Just as quickly as I had grown my lead, I gave one shot back. I didn't panic yet. A three-shot lead with four holes left was still a comfortable margin. All I had to do was hold it together for a few more holes.

At fifteen, a dogleg left, I hit a decent drive, but it drifted a little farther right than I wanted. I was surprised when I saw the ball stop in the rough, and I was shocked when I found it nestled in a deep divot—like an egg buried in the bottom of a nest. I had no chance of getting it on the green, and I wasn't even sure I could make contact.

After examining all my options and discussing the situation with my caddie, I took an iron and dug the ball out of its hole with a violent swing. As I expected, the low knuckleball shot landed in the bunker in front of the green. It was all I could do. Besides, the bunker wasn't that bad: I could still get the ball up and down for par, hopefully avoiding any damage to my lead.

As I was walking up to the bunker, I looked down at my right hand and saw that it was shaking...trembling like some pro-am rookie who had never won a two-dollar nassau. I cursed myself and put my hand in my pocket. I'd been nervous before. I thought that if you weren't a little bit nervous when you teed off in competition, you should give up the game. But I had always been able to channel nervousness to my advantage, using it to heighten my senses and give me an edge. This time, though, I was visibly shaking, something I hadn't done since I was a kid. It startled me at first, and I took a couple of deep breaths trying to calm my nerves and regain my focus. All I had to do was get up and down for par out of the bunker—something I'd done thousands of times in the past—then par sixteen, seventeen, and eighteen. I still had a three-shot lead. Just focus on the task at hand.

The bunker shot flew longer than I wanted and I left myself with a difficult twelve-foot putt for par. Normally, I would have relaxed, gone through my routine, and made a good aggressive stroke. But as I gripped the putter, I could see that my hand was still shaking. I tightened my grip in an effort to ward off the nerves overtaking me, and when I did, the putt never had a chance. I tapped in for bogey, and walked off the fifteenth green having given back another shot to the field.

I held a two-shot advantage with three holes to play...nothing to worry about...just par in and collect the victory. My damn hand just wouldn't stop shaking. I took three deep breaths, then a fourth, but I just couldn't calm my nerves. Mary Beth, playing first off the par-three sixteenth, hit her tee shot into the fringe, thirty feet from the hole. I breathed a little easier. Every golfer will tell you you're not supposed to play your opponent; you're supposed to play the golf course. But every *honest* golfer will also tell you that when things get tight down the stretch, it's impossible not to let your opponent's play affect your thinking. Mary Beth was the only player who had a ghost of a chance to catch me. So I felt a little more pumped up when she didn't hit it close on sixteen. My ball safely found the center of the green on sixteen, and then Mary Beth and I both two-putted for our pars.

I couldn't relax. At the seventeenth I had to take the little white tee out of my pocket with my left hand because my right hand was shaking so badly. As far as I could remember, nerves had never affected me like that. Even after I gripped the club, I could feel the nerves pulsing in my fingers, every tiny hair on the back of my hand standing at attention. One breath, two, then three, and finally I made a slow, deliberate swing with my driver. Once again the ball flew slightly to the right, but I didn't think it would be in any trouble. Maybe a little grass behind the ball in the light rough, but nothing too bad. After all, what were the odds of hitting it in another divot?

When I reached my ball and saw my predicament, I longed for another divot. As it was, I had a wonderful, fluffy, perched lie. But my ball sat right behind an evergreen pine seedling, about head-high, freshly planted, and held erect by a green rope anchored to stakes on three sides of its thin, fragile trunk. From my position I knew I was exactly 150 yards from the center of the green, but once again I had no chance of getting the ball anywhere close to the putting surface. My only shot was a half-swing punch that advanced the ball back into the fairway only marginally closer to the hole. From there I hit a decent approach to within ten feet, but with my hand shaking like mad, I missed my putt for par.

Mary Beth drove her ball in the fairway, but once again hit an average approach onto the green, twenty feet from the hole. Then lightning struck as Mary Beth rammed the twenty-foot birdie putt into the middle of the cup. A partial roar and palpable gasp went up from the crowd around the seventeenth green. What had once been an "insurmountable" lead was gone. Mary Beth and I were tied for the lead with one hole to play.

Apoplectic because of my boneheaded play, I marched onto the eighteenth tee, my lead gone and my hand shaking so badly that I wanted to cut it off at the wrist. Mary Beth and I hadn't said much to each other throughout the day. She was very quiet as a rule, and I didn't engage other players in a lot of conversation, either. As we headed to the par-three eighteenth, the tension had grown so thick that you could almost smell blood. Unfortunately, the bloodletting was mine. I had blown a lead that couldn't be blown, and now, with one hole to play, Mary Beth was poised for the kill, while I tried to calm my shaking hand long enough to hit a three-iron shot into the 178-yard par-three.

He poured a glass of white wine too full, and slid it over to me on a napkin. I gulped it like water, and the buttery smooth chill wet the glands of my throat like nectar from the gods.

Intent on not going right, I pulled my shot, yet it landed safely on the green about thirty feet from the hole. Mary Beth, who played first by virtue of her birdie, had already hit her shot ten feet from the hole. I hit my first putt so poorly that the ball ran twelve feet past. It was all I could do to breathe as I stood over the twelve-footer I had left myself for par, but somehow I made one of the best strokes of the day and the putt found the hole. It was too little too late. Mary Beth ran her ten-foot birdie putt squarely into the middle of the hole, and the tournament was over. She had birdied the last two holes, and I had played the last five holes in three over par—a five-shot swing in an hour and fifteen minutes.

At first I wanted to vomit, but I knew the television cameras were on, and I had to congratulate Mary Beth. She deserved it. Her play down the stretch was as gutsy as it was good. She had won the Uniden Invitational just as much as I had lost it, and I told her so. Then I went to the locker room where I put a towel over my face and wept. Several players and a few of my friends tried to console me, but I didn't want to speak to anyone. I didn't want anyone to see me, hear me, or even know that I existed. Dad couldn't make the trip to California, but he was standing by the phone, waiting for the news that his little girl had finally broken through on tour. When the call came, all he could say was, "Oh, no. Is she all right?"

I was anything but all right. The losses had mounted so high that I was consumed with doubt, fear, and questions about my future. Was I ever going to win? Did I have what it took? And what the hell was wrong with my hand? Even after Mary Beth had hoisted the trophy over her head at the postround ceremony, my hand still shook as it had throughout most of the final nine holes. I had no idea what could be causing this jittery behavior. Nervousness was one thing, but this was ridiculous.

After the tears dried and everyone else had left the club, I stuck around a little longer, not for memory's sake, but because I needed a drink before crawling into my red Porsche and making the drive south to Palm Springs. I sensed that the bar was officially closed, but the bartender recognized me, knew what had happened, and took pity on my plight. He poured a glass of white wine too full, and slid it over to me on a napkin. I gulped it like water, and the buttery smooth chill wet the glands of my throat like nectar from the gods. After finishing the glass in two swift slurps, I wiped the edges of my mouth and thanked the bartender. Then I looked down and noticed something. My hand had stopped shaking. Just like that. I held it up and turned it palm up, palm down; then I rolled my fingers in and out. Nothing. Not even a twitch. "Wonder what it could have been?" I asked myself as I headed out to my car and prepared for the long trip ahead.

CHAPTER *6*

WHAT'S A LOVE LIFE?

WHEN YOU'RE AN ALCOHOLIC working through a recovery program, your counselors require you to recount in detail your first drink, your last drink, and every drink along the way you can remember.

"When did alcohol first touch your lips? How did it taste? How did it make you feel? What did you think about drinking? How soon after your first drink did you have your second drink...your third drink...your fourth drink? When did you pour your first early-morning drink, and how did you rationalize it? When did you strike your first bargain with alcohol? When did you first say or think, 'I need a drink'?"

My last drinking episode, which landed me in the intensive care unit at the Sand Lake Medical Center a nanosecond from a date with the undertaker, was so dramatic that I had no trouble recalling every nuance in graphic detail. For the better part of a year prior to that episode, however, I operated in and out of blackouts and hallucinations where I would lose large chunks of time, waking up in obscure places with no recollection of how I had gotten there or what I had done. Sometimes I would be bruised. Sometimes I would be nude or wearing clothing I didn't remember putting on, and sometimes I would have to fumble for a phone book to find what city I was in.

Remembering those times was tough. People still recall things I did that I have no independent recollection of doing. I may never remember everything. If you made up the wildest story imaginable, I would have believed it. I never woke up in any sexually compromising positions, asking myself who the guy was next to me. I was just lucky. As for my first drink, I also remembered every nuance and detail surrounding it. I was twenty years old, and it was a screwdriver, ordered for me at dinner by the man I was convinced I would marry.

Unlike the image people had of me at the time, by my twentieth birthday I had barely dated, and my social life was virtually nonexistent. I didn't have time. Aside from traveling with the tour and playing an average of twenty-five tournaments a year, I spent every spare moment playing in corporate outings, traveling to various photo shoots, starring in television commercials, designing clothes, and sleeping on transpacific flights to Japan. For the first three years of my professional life, I celebrated Christmas, Thanksgiving, Easter, and my birthday alone on the road, dining at IHOP and sleeping in Holiday Inns. Granted, there was money everywhere, and despite my winless record, I was the most recognized golfer on the LPGA Tour; but success had its price. At times the loneliness became almost overbearing. Judy Rankin, Marlene Hagge, and Sandra Post were my best friends on tour, but we were competitors as well, trying to beat each other's brains out on the golf course. Friendships stayed in the clubhouse when we were playing, and when we weren't playing, I was away from home...alone...

Who loves short shorts? I did, especially at age nineteen. I've just crushed a drive at the 1974 LPGA Desert Inn Classic in Las Vegas. (CORBIS/BETTMAN-UPI)

tired…and trying to carve out some normalcy in an otherwise frenetic life.

It didn't take long for others to accuse me of greed, capitalizing on my looks and my name recognition to the detriment of my golf and at a cost to the women's game overall. That was nonsense then, and it is nonsense now. A player who capitalizes on his or her name and likeness while the popularity curve is still on an upswing is nothing short of a good businessperson.

Golfers are independent contractors who are paid for performance, so if I broke my hand or injured my back, my ability to make a living would disappear. Making money when I could was a smart move. As for the charge that one player's popularity somehow diminishes the game, I believe that anyone who broadens the public's awareness of women's professional sports helps everybody. More awareness translates into more fans, which in turn attracts more sponsors. Sponsors pay more for the right to associate with successful events and, as a result, purses go up, coverage is increased, and brand identity for the sport is enhanced.

It's a win-win situation today, just as it was back when I was doing my part to shine a spotlight on women's professional golf. Many of my fellow professionals didn't see things that way. Some said that my success came at the expense of others, as if every dollar I made was a dollar someone else didn't make. That "zero sum" mentality was as pervasive as it was wrong. When I brought exposure to the LPGA, everybody benefited from my exposure. During the years when I was seen as the "Golden Girl" of women's golf, tour purses were at record levels, and sponsors were knocking down doors trying to get involved in the women's game.

Feigning concern for my well-being, some of my peers said that IMG had gone overboard in exploiting me, running me ragged to the point where my golf suffered. That was silly. No one at IMG ever held a gun to my head, demanding I play in one extra corporate outing. They did a wonderful job of creating opportunities for me to make more money than anyone else in the women's game. Sometimes I said no to offers, and sometimes I said yes when I should have said no, but in any case the choices were mine and mine alone. I spent a lot of lonely hours on the road, because I chose to capitalize on my popularity before my fifteen minutes of fame expired. Just as no one ever tied me down and poured alcohol down my throat, no one ever strong-armed me into a commercial or an endorsement. I made my own decisions, good and bad.

One good decision I made in those early years was my choice of toothpaste. It wasn't as though I expended a great deal of energy on oral hygiene, but Ultra brite tasted good and kept my breath clean, so that's what I used. In my second year on tour at the Colgate Dinah Shore, marketing executives from Colgate canvassed the locker room in search of player-spokespeople. Company policy stated that only those players who used Colgate products would be offered sponsorship agreements. Ultra brite, as luck would have it, was Colgate's premier whitening toothpaste. In short order, I became the Ultra brite Girl, and within weeks I was in Los Angeles shooting a television commercial.

"Hey, Laura Baugh, how's your love life?" an off-camera voice asked.

I twirled around and answered, "What's a love life?"

Then there was a product shot with an off-camera voice extolling the many virtues of brushing your pearly whites with tube after tube of Ultra brite. On camera, I squeezed a dab of paste onto my index finger and rubbed it across my upper incisors, face aglow from the wondrous taste of Ultra brite. Then, as if he had popped out of the toothpaste tube like a genie, a gorgeous male model appeared, and we cautiously embraced.

That little miracle of Madison Avenue took a full day and a pound of toothpaste to shoot. A year later, Colgate won a Clio (advertising's equivalent to the Emmys and the Academy Awards) for the Ultra brite ad, and a who's who of advertising turned out for a black-tie ceremony in New York to see my smiling face on a big screen, saying for the millionth time, "What's a love life?"

It was meant to be funny, but when I uttered that line, I wasn't making it up. Laura Baugh didn't have a love life, and given my workload, I had no clue when I was going to fit one into my schedule. Not that I wasn't interested, I just didn't have time. I wanted a meaningful relationship, but I still bore the scars of my parents' nasty breakup, so I refused to rush into anything. My husband would be a life partner, the father of all the children I wanted to have, and the soul mate like my mother had longed for but somehow hadn't found. I wanted a family, a husband I could count on to love and provide, and children—lots of children. By the time I was twenty, I was a three-year veteran of the tour with a substantial financial nest egg. In keeping with my original plan when I turned down Stanford's scholarship offer, I could play for a decade and still be in my twenties with ample time for another career and a family. Running across the right man was the only kink in the plan.

Having lived through the high-decibel scenes my parents inflicted on us, I then suffered my mother's bitter vindictiveness. I knew better than most how a seemingly stable relationship could disintegrate. That wasn't going to happen to me. I was going to be careful and sure before I got serious with anyone. By virtue of my early celebrity, I also knew how difficult it was to meet people when you worked thirteen-hour days and traveled to a different city every week. There were plenty of fans, plenty of people who wanted to get to know me without really getting to know me, and plenty of sycophantic young boys who thought dating a well-known golfer would be cool. I needed someone who understood my career, my goals, my lifestyle, and my dreams.

My husband would be a life partner, the father of all the children I wanted to have, and the soulmate like my mother had longed for but somehow hadn't found.

I thought I'd found that person when I met Bobby Cole.

✦ ✦ ✦

In June 1975 I was scheduled to travel to Geneva to play in Bruce Rappaport's Intermaritime International Pro-Am, the biggest pro-am event in the world, which attracted Europe's most renowned business executives, as well as professionals (both men and women) from all tours. I was scheduled to play in the same event in 1974, but right before I was to fly to Europe, one of my wisdom teeth abscessed, and my dentist recommended that I have all four wisdom teeth removed. Unfortunately, that decision killed my golf for a week, and I couldn't make the trip to the Rappaport event. My agent at the time, Hughes Norton, was not pleased. "You have to go. *You've committed!*" Norton shouted when I called him.

Had I not been lying in bed with my jaw packed full of gauze, I would have ripped into Norton. As it was, I could barely sit upright, so lecturing my agent on the virtues of proper decorum would have to wait. "I'm sorry, Hughes," I mumbled. "Send them my sincerest apologies and I promise I'll play next year, even if I'm on my deathbed."

Good to my word, I made the trip to Geneva the next year for what proved to be a rewarding experience. Lanny Wadkins, also an IMG client at the time, made the trip as well. Although Lanny and I had been good friends since my rookie year on tour, romance was never a part of our relationship, despite persistent rumors to the contrary. We were buddies, but a lot of people misinterpreted our friendship, assuming we were dating. One of them was Bobby Cole, a South African professional of twenty-seven and a man Mark McCormack once called "the most talented golfer" he'd ever seen. I knew of Bobby because he had occasionally dated Sally Little, a fellow South African who had great success on the LPGA Tour. When he played in the group behind me in Geneva, I didn't know who he was, but I thought he had one of the most beautiful golf swings I'd ever seen. After our round, I sought him out and told him exactly that. "Hi, I'm Laura Baugh," I said, hand outstretched.

"Bobby Cole," he said, taking my hand in a firm but gentle grip. He held on a moment longer than my instincts told me he should, but I couldn't help returning his handsome and infectious smile. Maybe this was a sign. Maybe there was something here that I needed to explore.

I said, "You have the most beautiful golf swing I've ever seen."

He laughed, and I laughed with him. I felt something click. He might have believed that Lanny and I were an item at the time, and I wasn't sure what his relationship was with Sally, but I knew I had to learn more about this man. For months thereafter, I did my best to investigate everything I could about South African golf star Bobby Cole.

My sleuthing turned up that Bobby and Sally were no longer together, and as far as anyone in golf knew, he was unattached. I was from the old school, and it was unconscionable for me to consider asking him out. Men were supposed to ask women out. It was his job to call me. He was supposed to properly court me: take me to dinner, pay for the meal, drive the car, open the door for me, be a gentleman, and advance the notion that we should see each other again. But with Bobby playing the men's tour and me traveling the globe for endorsements when I wasn't playing the LPGA Tour, the only time I was likely to see him again was on the practice range at the next year's Rappaport Pro-Am. That would never do. Somehow I was going to have to expedite the process.

The opportunity came in August 1975 when, by fate, I was scheduled to spend a few days in David Crystal's New York design studios at the same time the PGA Tour event was played at nearby Westchester Country Club. Mom made the trip with me, and after squeezing in two solid days of work in the fashion studio, we rented a car and drove to Westchester. I was a little concerned about appearing too anxious, but Mom assured me that following Bobby around the golf course was not only proper, it was expected protocol in the pre-dating ritual. The fire-engine red shorts she insisted I wear were insurance. If the gallery was big, we had to make sure Bobby noticed me.

He did. After the seventeenth hole, Bobby's caddie, Norman Martin, said to him, "Why don't you go over and ask Laura out?"

"Do you think I should?" he asked.

Norman said, "Well, she's been following you for seventeen holes, and I don't think it's because of your stellar golf."

Bobby agreed, and on the eighteenth tee he walked over to the gallery ropes where we were standing. That ear-to-ear smile led him everywhere he went, and I beamed in acknowledgment. After some brief niceties and an obligatory introduction to Mom, Bobby asked if I cared to join him for dinner. I shrugged as if the idea had never occurred to me. "Sure," I said in a passive way. After all, we both have to eat.

We were staying in a guesthouse near the club, so after his round Bobby came by and picked me up and we dined at the club that evening. As the host was seating us, Bobby turned to me and asked, "What do you want to drink?"

"I...I don't know," I said through a sheepish grin. "You order for me."

He gave me another smile and said, "Do you like screwdrivers?"

I had to assume he was referring to a drink and not a household tool. I had never had a screwdriver or any other drink, so I had no idea if I liked it or not. "Sure, whatever," I answered with a slight wave of my hand. I assumed sophisticated drinkers gave those sorts of curt

Overseas travel was old hat for me by the time I was twenty. Here I am lining up a putt during a pro-am event preceding the 1974 Colgate European Open in Sunning-dale, England. A year later back at Sunningdale I had more reason to smile, thanks to a telegram from Bobby that greeted me when I arrived. (CORBIS/BETTMAN-UPI)

hand gestures and, more than anything, I wanted Bobby to think I was sophisticated, a worldly and intelligent date, worthy of future consideration.

When the drink arrived, I smiled, thanked the waiter, and sipped it from a straw. It tasted like old transmission fluid. At first I puckered and considered spitting the vile liquid back into the glass. That would have been an ice-breaker. I finally willed the muscles of my throat to swallow, and I did my best to smile while suppressing a gag reflex. Without missing a conversational beat, I gingerly slid the glass to the center of the table and didn't touch another drop.

Bobby had a tough weekend at Westchester, shooting 76-74 in the final two rounds to finish in a disappointing tie for sixtieth. I, on the other hand, couldn't have been happier. By all objective measures, the date was a success. He had paid for the meal, been the perfect gentleman, driven me back to the guesthouse, and kissed me on the cheek as we said our good-byes.

Monday of the following week I flew to London to play in the Colgate European Open at Sunningdale Golf Club in Berkshire. When I arrived at my hotel, I had a telegram waiting. My heart skipped a beat as I opened it and read, "Good luck. Play well. Love, Bobby."

"Love, Bobby." It was a sign. Could this be the one? I carefully folded the telegram, put it into my purse, and proceeded to have a great week of golf in London. When I returned home, I would somehow get a message to him, thanking him again for the date and the note. This might develop into something great. And it might not.

✦ ✦ ✦

I didn't need to float any messages through the golf grapevine. Bobby called almost immediately. He came to Delray Beach to visit me at the Hamlet, and we began dating regularly. The remainder of 1975 and the early part of 1976, I saw Bobby exclusively. Everyone in golf knew we were together, and everyone assumed we would be married. I certainly believed it. After a solid eight months of dating, I was completely confident that a white dress and wedding bells were in my future. Bobby would be my partner for life.

By April 1976 I was certain that he was on the brink of proposing. He invited me to come to Augusta to watch him play in the Masters. I knew that was going to be the week. Augusta in the springtime is a magical place, full of life and color and turn-of-the-century romance, the perfect setting for a man to propose to the woman he loves. I would be staying in a rented house near Augusta National Golf Club with Bobby, Peter Oosterhuis, and Bobby's regular caddie, Norman Martin.

It was a quiet five-mile ride from the airport to the house, but in that time I began rationalizing why he hadn't bothered coming to meet me.

Logistics proved a minor inconvenience. The week before the Masters, the LPGA held its first major championship of the year, the Dinah Shore Classic, in Palm Springs. Judy Rankin won the tournament, and I played well, tied for thirteenth with Sandra Palmer and Gloria Ehret. After the final putt fell on Sunday, I hopped into my Thunderbird and sped north to Los Angeles where I barely made the last red-eye flight out of LAX bound for Hartsfield International in Atlanta. I was always a nervous flier, so sleep was out of the question. When we landed in Atlanta, I sprinted through the airport to make my connecting commuter flight to Augusta. I'd been up all night after playing golf all day, and I was exhausted. The thought of what awaited me in Augusta kept me going, though. I tidied my makeup during the commuter flight to Bush Field in Augusta, and when the plane touched down, I felt a surge of adrenaline rush though my body. This was it.

My face was numb from lack of sleep, but I couldn't wait to get off the plane and jump into Bobby's arms. I skipped down the ramp, scanning the crowd. When I didn't spot him right away, I glanced around the terminal. Maybe he had the wrong gate? Maybe he had gone to the rest room just as the plane was landing? I was sure he was there somewhere. Then I saw Norman Martin sitting in a chair near the gate. "Norman?" I said.

"Oh, hi, Laura. Did you have a good flight?"

"Where's Bobby?"

"He was asleep at the house when I left. Where are your bags?"

"Asleep!"

I couldn't believe it. I had played the final round of a major championship, hopped into a car, and driven like a maniac for three hours to fly across the country without so much as a nap, and he couldn't get his fanny out of bed to meet me at the airport! Unacceptable!

It was a quiet five-mile ride from the airport to the house, but in that time I began rationalizing why he hadn't bothered coming to meet me. No doubt he had arrived in Augusta late the night before, and he *did* have a practice round that Monday, and the Masters *was* the grandest prize in all of men's golf. He needed to focus. He needed to rest. It wasn't a slight against me in any way. By the time we pulled into the driveway, I had completely forgiven him. After all, this was the week he was going to propose.

Monday's practice round came and went, as did Tuesday's. Bobby was his usual delightful self, smiling and playing the role of the gentleman. We went to the club early so we could drink in all the sights and sounds that make the

Masters a unique experi-
ence. I couldn't believe it
was the same golf course I
had sneaked through only
four years earlier when I
was next door playing the
U.S. Junior Girls. Every-
thing seemed so much big-
ger, brighter, and more
stately during the Masters.
We watched golf, had food
delivered and prepared at
the house, chatted with
friends—a delightful time.
But Bobby gave no sign
that he was in the mood to
propose marriage. After
the tournament officially
began on Thursday, I duti-

Bobby (Cole) in a pensive moment. He was a terrific amateur golfer, although his pro career never panned out for various reasons—which was pretty much the story of our two marriages as well. (LAURA BAUGH)

fully walked every step of every round, just like Barbara
Nicklaus and Winnie Palmer and the other tour wives. But I
wasn't a tour wife, and despite what I thought were perfect
circumstances, it didn't look as though I would become one
any time soon.

Bobby shot a final-round 82 and finished dead last out
of those players who made the weekend cut at the Masters.
He did win some nice crystal for a couple of eagles he made
early in the week, but I found little consolation in that.
Dejected, I returned home to the Hamlet where I took a
week off before heading to Birmingham, Alabama, the next
stop on the LPGA Tour.

We continued dating when our schedules allowed, but things were different after Augusta. I was now a four-year veteran of the tour, and I wanted to get married and start a family. By fall 1976, I had my doubts about Bobby ever feeling the same way. When the men's tour returned to Florida in November for the Walt Disney World Team Championship, I drove to Orlando, had dinner with Bobby, and gave him an ultimatum.

"I want to get married," I said. "I want to be a married person, and I want to have children. You say that you love me, and I certainly love you, so what's the holdup? We've been dating for a year. You need to commit to me or this isn't going to work."

After a fair amount of hemming and hawing in his thick South African brogue, Bobby said, "Sorry. I would love to. I just can't."

It was like a dagger through my heart. Wounded to the core, I went home and cried for days. Bobby had been the one, but something I had done, some part of my personality, kept him from loving me enough to marry me. It had to be my fault. If I had only loved him more, maybe he would have proposed under the oak tree behind the old plantation clubhouse in Augusta, or maybe he would have said yes in Orlando. Maybe if I had done more, committed more, been there for him more often, he would have found me worthy of marrying. How could I be so unappealing? What could I have possibly done to drive him away?

Those questions were almost too painful to ponder. He had turned me down. I returned to the Hamlet and went out with the first man who asked me.

That turned out to be the biggest mistake of my life.

CHAPTER 7

CHOICES

I'LL CALL HIM WILL ROSS, although that is not his real name. He was an assistant golf pro at the Hamlet, not a very lucrative position, but stable—just what I needed after being jilted by Bobby in such heartbreaking fashion. Will was always around. He was in the golf shop or on the lesson tee when I was home in Delray Beach, and we would exchange pleasantries. He seemed nice enough—big, handsome, rugged—with a maverick sort of wildness so vastly different from Bobby that I found him appealing. His background was a bit of a mystery, but that only added to the attraction for a young, impressionable twenty-three-year-old on the rebound. When he asked me out to dinner, I accepted without hesitation.

After the debacle with the screwdriver, Bobby and I occasionally drank wine with dinner, and I acquired a moderate taste for white wine and champagne. At that time Bobby and I were both into strong fitness regimens, so drinking didn't fit our schedules. A little wine with dinner was about as wild as we got. Will, on the other hand, drank big time. On our first date he ordered cocktails before dinner (I had wine), two bottles of Chablis with dinner, and a couple of glasses of Piesporter for dessert. He fancied himself a connoisseur of fine wine, and he would often launch into charming lectures on the flavor and bouquet of certain vintages.

His taste didn't end with wine, however. Will drank bourbon, Scotch, vodka, rum, and all combinations thereof, but he never fell down, never got sloppy, and never fell asleep at the dinner table. He was a big man who partied big, drank big, and had, I thought, a big heart. Three hours into our first dinner together, Will asked me to marry him. I laughed, but I couldn't help but be struck by the difference between this man and the one I had just left. Bobby and I dated each other for a year, and the very mention of marriage sent him into a cold sweat. Will wanted to get married after the first date.

I turned him down, but that didn't stop him. Will and I dated for months. He was fun, and I was young and into an exploratory stage of my life. It was the late seventies, when disco and Studio 54 were all the rage, and I was a twenty-three-year-old, reasonably well-off, marginally attractive woman with no commitments and no ties. Will was a partying sort of guy who loved to stay out late, drink, and dance the night away. It was the perfect seventies relationship—glitzy, superficial, and blurred by the haze of alcohol.

Throughout most of 1977 and 1978, Will and I dated, and during that time I felt sure I would marry him. I wanted to get married and start a family, and Will was a nice, stable guy. I never had to travel to him, never had to catch the red-eye only to be abandoned at the airport, and never had to wonder when he was going to ask me to marry him. He did that every time we were together.

I enjoyed the good life, splitting time between Florida and Palm Springs, playing in fifty-four events over a twenty-four-month period and finishing in the top twenty-five on the money list both years. There were party friends on the West Coast and on the East Coast, and at every tour stop in between. Throughout it all, Will was there, calling and saying things like, "I miss you...I'd love to see you."

I loved the flattery. Will wanted to marry me so much, he would drive a thousand miles just to spend one night with me, and that was something I'd never experienced. He seemed lovable enough. Certainly, he had no lack of words to express how much he cared for me. We became engaged, and I flew to New York and picked out a wedding dress and bridesmaids' gowns. Finally, after a year of dating a man who wouldn't marry me, I had found someone who worshiped me. It didn't matter that he earned less than I did or that he wasn't as financially stable. We were in love. That was all that mattered.

When Will called and asked if he could come to Hilton Head to watch me play in the Women's International, I didn't hesitate. Dad was going to be there with his girlfriend, so it seemed like a perfect opportunity for the four of us to spend time together. Everything went according to plan until the first night we all went out to dinner. As usual, Will ordered before-dinner drinks, during-dinner drinks, after-dinner drinks, and then we went out for a couple of drinks and a dance or two before bedtime. I had to play the next day, so Will and I returned early to our rented condo. It was there that the trouble started.

Will could be as charming and persuasive as anyone I had ever been around, until he got drunk. When he got drunk, he turned nasty, and when he turned nasty, he lashed out in violent ways. By that time I had learned he'd been married once before and he had a daughter. Details were sketchy, but from what he told me, he wasn't allowed to visit his daughter. I never knew why, but it didn't take long for me to narrow the possibilities. As the two of us embraced in the bedroom of our rented condo at Moss Creek Plantation on Hilton Head, Will started asking questions about other men I knew from my travels on tour. None of these guys were romantic liaisons. But Will had trouble differentiating between friendship and romantic friendship. "Are you still talking to Mickey in Denver? How about John in Wisconsin?" he asked.

I answered truthfully, a big mistake. "Yes, I occasionally speak to Mickey in Denver," I said.

Whap!

He slapped me, and I stumbled over the nearby dresser. For a moment I was dazed. *What has happened?* The room turned suddenly bright, then instantly dark. Pain flooded the side of my face.

"What about John in Wisconsin? Do you still talk to him?"

Whap!

Another blow, and I hit the floor. It took me a couple of seconds to catch my breath and, in that time, I realized that he was right over me. I had to think. There had to be something I could say to make him stop. Then it came to me. Facing the floor, my head throbbing in pain, I said, "You had better get out of here before my dad gets back. If he sees this, he'll annihilate you."

Saying what I did was risky. What if he freaked out at the threat I'd just made? He could kill me before anyone heard me scream. I cringed and waited for the next blow, but it never came. He silently stormed out of the room, and I finally took a deep breath.

That was it. I would press charges and have the psycho banned from coming anywhere near me. This tryst was over. I wouldn't tolerate being hit.

The next morning, as I was preparing to tee off at Moss Creek's Devil's Elbow course in what sponsors considered the LPGA Tour's equivalent to the Masters, Will tracked me down. At first I was frightened, but as he talked, his voice quivering and on the verge of tears, my fear turned to compassion.

Facing the floor, my head throbbing in pain, I said, "You had better get out of here before my dad gets back. If he sees this, he'll annihilate you."

"I'm so sorry," he begged. "Please forgive me. It's just that I'm so jealous, and I love you so much. I swear it will never happen again. You're so beautiful. I just can't bear the thought of anyone else being with you. I want to marry you and love you forever. You know that. It's all I've ever wanted. I was drunk last night. You know I would never do anything to hurt you."

After a few minutes of listening, I felt sorry for him and what he'd gone through. It wasn't really his fault that he hit me. We had all been drinking, and I understood how he could misconstrue my other friendships. It was certainly understandable…reasonable even. He just had trouble expressing himself. It would never happen again. He'd promised. It was silly of me to consider calling the police. After all, he loved me. Why would I want to push away someone who loved me?

✦ ✦ ✦

Will's promise held true for seven weeks. During that time, he couldn't have been more pleasant and fun to be around. We went out, drank, and danced. When he asked if he could come to Detroit to watch me play in the Lady Stroh's Open, I welcomed him with open arms. The first night of the tournament, we went out to dinner and drank a couple of bottles of wine. We were in love, wine flowed freely, and life was beautiful.

I was nude when the phone in my room rang. It was a good friend of mine from California, a happily married man. He had called to wish me well and offer me his good thoughts going into the tournament. I thanked him, and we hung up.

"Who was that?" Will asked in a voice that had gone frighteningly cold.

When I told him, I assumed that would be the end of it. The next thing I knew, Will's fist came toward me, and the room that had been full of air suddenly became a vacuum. There had to be air out there somewhere, but I couldn't inhale. I fell on the bed and bent over, willing myself to gulp what little oxygen I could find. Then something sharp struck the back of my head. At first I thought it was a knife. I kept waiting for the sick sound of tearing flesh, but it never came. A second later I looked up in time to see the dagger-like heel of my left shoe hurtling toward my eye. I flinched and the shoe caught the bone between my eye socket and my temple. I thought I was blind, but then I realized the pain was isolated to the side of my face. When the warmth started trickling down my cheek, I knew I'd been cut. I leaned over and tucked my head in my arms, but that didn't stop the attack. Will started slashing my shoulders with the heel of the shoe, shouting and grunting with every blow. At first I tried to stagger away, but that only made him angrier. I knew I needed to outsmart him or he would beat me to death with my own shoe.

The idea came to me as Will tried to drive the heel of the shoe into my spinal cord between the fourth and fifth vertebra. If I could distract him, maybe I could get out of the room and get some help. "Oh, my God, look," I screamed, as I pointed toward the window. "Somebody's out there watching."

He stormed over to the window, dropping the shoe and throwing back the curtains, his eyes darting from side to side. That was the break I needed. With his back turned, I leapt for the door and didn't look back. Naked and bleeding, I ran down four flights of stairs. I could hear him behind me, two, maybe three flights up. I was taking the stairs two at a time in bare feet when I darted through a door and headed around a corner and down a carpeted hallway. I starting banging on the first door I saw. A man in pajamas cracked the door slightly.

"Please help me," I cried. Blood had started to cake around my eye, and my back and head were starting to swell. The man hesitated for a second. "Please," I insisted. "He's chasing me."

The man didn't need to know who "he" was to figure out what had happened. He let me in the room and quickly retrieved a towel from the bathroom. After covering myself, I dialed the switchboard for Sandra Post's room. I knew Sandra was in the hotel, but I had no idea where. She had been in Hilton Head when the first incident took place, and every player and caddie at the event knew what had happened. Fortunately, the press never got wind of it, and as is often the case in the fickle world of professional golf, by the next week it had become old news on tour. Still, Sandra was a friend who knew about Will's temper. If I could get to her room, I would be safe. *Come on, answer the phone,* I willed her after the third ring.

"Hello."

Sandra sounded like she had been asleep. "Sandra, it's Laura. What room are you in?"

"Huh?"

"What room are you in? What room?"

She told me and I hung up.

"Are you all right?" the man in the room asked as I headed toward the door.

"Thank you," I said. "I'll think I'll be fine."

I wished I believed that. The truth was I didn't know what Will would do if he found me. At that moment, I had to get to Sandra's room. Somehow I knew I would be safe there.

She was waiting at the door when I arrived. "Oh, my God," Sandra exclaimed. "Where is he?" she asked.

"I don't know," I said. "Probably on his way here once he realizes that you're in the hotel."

Sandra deadbolted the door, then ran warm water onto a washcloth and pressed it against my head. Two minutes later there was a thunderous pounding on the door. "Laura. I know you're in there. I need to talk to you!" Will bellowed. "I just want to talk, Laura. Come on, I'm not going to hurt you."

"Get out of here, Will!" Sandra shouted.

"Come on, Laura. I just want to talk."

"I'm calling the cops right now, Will," Sandra said loudly. "They'll be here in five minutes, less if I tell them you're armed."

I couldn't believe how gutsy she was. When I look back on that incident now, I realize what a hero Sandra Post is. No matter how golf historians recall her accomplishments, I will always remember the night she saved my life. But I wasn't smart enough to listen to the advice she gave me after Will stopped banging on the door.

"Get away from him, Laura," she warned. "He's dangerous, and he's going to hurt you really bad, maybe worse. At the very least, he's going to kill your career. Just get away."

"I know he is," I sobbed. "I know. He was drunk. We'd been to dinner."

"Don't make excuses for him," she snapped. "He hit you, for God's sake. This is serious. He's not going to get better."

Somewhere in my mind I knew Sandra was right, but when Will showed up at the Dearborn Country Club the next morning, he seemed to be a changed man. By the time Will arrived, the LPGA grapevine had been hard at work. Most of the players and all of the caddies knew what had happened, and the caddies were livid. I wore sunglasses and tried to cover up the injuries with an extra-heavy application of makeup, but I couldn't hide the obvious. Before Will came near me, a group of caddies cornered him and discussed his behavior in terms that he understood and took to heart. As I was standing on the putting green, he sheepishly came over, flanked on both sides by loyal male members of the LPGA Tour caddie corps.

"You can call the cops and press charges if you want," he said. "God knows, I deserve it. I just want you to know how sorry I am. I can't believe I did this. I'm sorry."

The "I love you" part didn't come for another couple of weeks but, like clockwork, he called. He loved me, you see, but he was insecure, and that insecurity sometimes manifested itself in jealousy. Occasionally (only when he drank), the jealousy would overwhelm him, and because he didn't know any other way of expressing himself, he would hit. Of course it was boorish, but he only did it because he loved me, you see. If he didn't love me, he wouldn't have cared enough to beat me senseless. Yes, it was wrong, but he understood it was wrong, and if I would only marry him, he would be a whole person. The insecurities would vanish and Will Ross would be transformed from a batterer into a kind, loving husband and provider. He had learned from his history, you see. All I had to do was marry him, and life would be better for the both of us.

I left Will and began dating other men, among them singer and actor Mac Davis. My days of serious commitment were over for awhile. I partied long and hard, going out in Palm Springs at midnight and dancing until four or five in the morning. Then I would work on my golf and go out again. I wasn't interested in being serious with anyone—I was zip-for-two on the boyfriend front. The shallowness of that lifestyle never hit me until I was alone on the road. In hotel rooms, dining by myself, the pain of loneliness would sometimes drive me to tears. It was always in those weak moments that Will would call. "No one will ever love you the way I love you, Laura," he would say. "I can't live without you. We should always be together. I promise I will always be there for you."

✦ ✦ ✦

Will and I were married in a small Episcopal chapel in Denton, Texas, just north of Dallas, on New Year's Eve 1979. My mother and father refused to attend, but my brother Hale stood by my side in the quaint, quick ceremony I finally consented to. Things had gotten much better by then. After my endorsement deal with the Hamlet expired, I bought a ranch-style house on five acres in Argyle, Texas. Because of the tax laws and the fact that Dallas was centrally located with a decent climate and a good airport, many professionals from the PGA and LPGA Tours chose to live there. I still had a condo at Mission Hills in California, so the Texas residence suited my needs perfectly. I could travel out of Dallas and play in twenty-five to thirty events a year, and when the Texas weather was uncooperative, I would retreat to California for a few months.

By flaunting my sexuality with things like lipstick and mascara, I was taunting him. It was my fault.

Before I ever consented to marry him, Will changed careers and moved to Dallas to be near me. He could make me feel like a princess, and the hitting had stopped, so I finally gave in to his persistence. After all, I wanted to be married, and I wanted a family, and Will certainly wanted to marry me. At age twenty-five, I was ready to start a new life in the 1980s.

After our wedding, we celebrated by drinking more champagne than I normally consumed in a year. Then we went back to my house in Argyle for a quiet at-home honey-moon. I traveled all the time, so going away on a honey-moon wasn't particularly appealing. We said good-bye to the handful of guests who had come to the service and ventured to our new home as Mr. and Mrs. Will Ross. We drank more champagne at home and exchanged gifts. I had bought him a Rolex, and he had found a beautiful gold bracelet for me. The house was perfect for raising a family, and now that I was married, I hoped to start having kids immediately.

I'm not sure what triggered it, but as our wedding night progressed, it became obvious that Will's dark side was creeping to the surface. I must have said something that sent him over the edge, although I have no idea what it was. I remember being hit. I shouted and fell. He grabbed me by the hair, dragged me through the house, and forced me onto the bed. I tried to get away.

My heart sank when I looked into the black abyss of his eyes—the eyes of a monster. He was on top of me, holding me down, and threatening me. I knew at that moment that he was going to kill me. Maybe not that night, maybe not that week or that month, but someday I was going to die by his hand. Of that there was no question. It was an awakening. All the warnings from the players, from my family, from my agents, and from my friends came flooding to my mind, and I realized with pristine clarity that they had all been right. "He's bad news, Laura," was about the kindest thing my dad ever said about him. Alastair Johnston, a native of Glasgow and a longtime friend from IMG who managed Arnold Palmer's affairs, had said in his thick Scottish brogue that Will "wasn't quite top shelf." Then there were the women on tour who told me to get far, far away

My expression here belies what I was going through at the time. It is between practice rounds at a 1976 tournament in Miami, and I have just asked for police protection from a male stalker who had been following me for more than two months and had threatened me. I guess this was a precursor to the real violence I would experience two years later in my first marriage. (AP/WIDE WORLD PHOTOS)

from him. Now, I knew what they meant. I was a fool for thinking he would change. So what if he promised not to hit me again? The fact that he hit me in the first place was enough. I should have had him arrested the first time he touched me. Hilton Head, Detroit—the warnings were clear, but I believed him when he said that he loved me, when he said it was only jealousy and that marriage would solve all our problems. Now as he was lying on top of me, pulling my hair, hitting me, threatening me, all those rationalizations had come back to haunt me. I would die because I had fallen for the oldest line in the book: "I love you, Laura. That's why I beat you."

I closed my eyes and let him have his way with me. For years I blocked out the details of that night, choosing to forget it rather than deal with the fact that I married a madman. I still have trouble remembering a lot of what happened, but I do recall ending up outside, nude, covered only with a blanket, in the gutter that lined the street in front of my house. I laid motionless in the gutter throughout most of the night. When I was sure Will was asleep, I sneaked back in and slept on the couch in the living room. The next morning there was a flood of tears and apologies like never before.

Now that we were married, my makeup was the problem. If I wouldn't wear makeup and make myself attractive to other men, then he wouldn't fly into such a jealous rage. By flaunting my sexuality with things like lipstick and mascara, I was taunting him. It was my fault. If only I would change...be better...be less attractive to other men...have dinner prepared on time more often...keep the house a bit cleaner, then things would be all right.

For the first three weeks of January, I remained a prisoner in my own home. I couldn't call anyone, couldn't wear makeup, and couldn't go anywhere. My days consisted of cleaning the house, making a two-mile trip to the grocery store, a couple of hours of golf at Denton Country Club, and dinner on the table promptly at 6:30. "Don't be gone too long," he would say. To get through it, I would drink a beer with my Wheaties in the morning and upgrade to wine by early afternoon. This was my first retreat into alcohol. Wine helped ease the tension, calm the fear, and numb the reality that I was trapped in a horrific cycle of violence and abuse. It was the first time I needed to drink to shut out the world around me.

I should have had the marriage annulled. Certainly, if I had been more mature, that's what I would have done. I actually believed some of it was my fault. I drank when Will drank. I had no excuse. I knew what he was capable of long before I walked down the aisle with him. I was as much to blame as anyone. Of course, now I know that was the classic battered-woman response, a warning sign of obsessive behavior. I didn't notice.

The last week of January, I went back out on tour as a woman reprieved. I knew I would never stay married to Will, but I made no immediate attempt to end the marriage, even though I never spent another night in the house in Argyle. I couldn't stay married to Will, not if I wanted to live. Weeks dragged into months. A few times Will came out on tour for a day or two, but those instances were rare. He never stopped apologizing, always promising it would never happen again.

Finally, in the summer, after the West Virginia LPGA Classic in Wheeling, I mustered enough courage to initiate action. I called Alastair Johnston in Cleveland. "Alastair, I want to get a divorce," I said without much preamble.

Alastair didn't know all that had happened in my marriage, but he knew Will, and he knew my decision was long overdue. He suggested we meet in Pittsburgh to discuss the details of my decision, so I got into my rented car and drove to the Pittsburgh airport hotel where I filled him in on all the sordid details of my life with Will.

It didn't take long for Alastair to get the ball rolling. We spent one night in Pittsburgh, then flew together to Dallas, where Alastair and I met with a group of lawyers who worked closely with IMG. The conference was longer and more uncomfortable than I expected, primarily because the group of well-dressed lawyerly gentlemen wanted to know every intimate detail of my marriage to Will, especially the bad stuff. After a couple of hours, one of the older counselors in the group said, "Laura, divorce is not going to be easy, especially given your assets and your prominence. You need to think about this. Why don't you go out for an hour or so and talk it over with Alastair, then come back and tell us what you've decided."

It was a muggy, hot afternoon in downtown Dallas. Alastair and I bought ice cream from a street vendor and sat on a park bench adjacent to Dealey Plaza. Alastair asked, "Are you sure this is what you want to do?" I had never been so sure of anything in my entire life, and I told him so. "Fine," he said. "Let's go get things started."

That afternoon I signed the paperwork in Dallas Municipal Court to begin divorce proceedings against Will Ross. It was finally over. I could put the nightmare behind me. There were some things in the house I needed to retrieve, however, the most important being a little Yorkshire terrier named Wilson. I asked Alastair if he would accompany me to the house, and he reluctantly agreed. It was unspoken, but both of us knew that if Will saw the two of us together, he would assume all sorts of crazy things, and with his temper anything could happen.

As we drove north out of town, I suddenly saw a white sedan coming toward us.

"Oh, my God," I said.

"What is it?" Alastair asked.

At that moment the car passed us and I saw him. "That was Will who just passed us," I said. "Pull over. We've got to pull over."

Oh, God, what else could go wrong?

Alastair pulled the car behind a cluster of trees, and the two of us got out and hid in some nearby brush where we could see the road. It was chigger season in Texas, and the tiny invisible insects immediately attacked my ankles. Alastair was in a coat and tie, probably wondering what he had gotten himself into. When we were certain Will hadn't seen us, we got back in the car and drove to my house. That's when I made what proved to be another grave error.

After retrieving Wilson and stowing him in a small kennel to carry onto the plane, I went into the kitchen and wrote a note: "Will, I have just filed for divorce and I'm leaving town. The lawyers will be in touch soon. Until then, do not try to contact me. Laura." I left it on the table where I knew he would find it and went back to the car where Alastair was waiting, the engine running for a quick getaway.

"You did what?" Alastair said after I told him about the note.

"I needed to tell him something," I said.

"Laura, if he finds that note, don't you think he's going to come looking for you?"

Will knew I would be headed to my condo in Palm Springs, and depending on how ballistic he went when he read that note, I could be in danger. The lawyers said the divorce would take a minimum of thirty days if everything went uncontested. Will wasn't likely to go away uncontested. At that moment, I just hoped I would live to see it through.

Alastair drove straight to DFW Airport where he booked his flight for Cleveland, and I bought a ticket to Los Angeles. We had about an hour before either flight boarded, so we went upstairs to a bar that overlooked the terminal. We sat at a table near the large window, and when the waiter brought my wine, I chugged half the glass in one gulp. When I looked at Alastair, I could see his face had gone pale.

"Oh, my god, there's Will," he said.

"Where?" I shouted, turning to look out the window at the terminal below.

"Don't—" Alastair started to say, but it was too late. A burly figure wearing a cowboy hat and boots stopped in his tracks and looked up. Our eyes met, and I could see the fury on Will's face. He had found us. I thought about running, but Alastair assured me he wouldn't try anything foolish in an airport bar. I wasn't so sure. Nothing he did surprised me.

"Laura, I need to talk to you."

Now he was standing over our table, his chest heaving, his face flushed and red. I focused on his trembling hand; I couldn't bring myself to look at him. If he was going to hit me in the Dallas airport, I refused him the satisfaction of seeing fear in my eyes.

"I just want to talk to you," he said again.

"Laura, I don't see why you can't at least talk to Will," Alastair said in his most conciliatory tone. I didn't know if my knees would support me, but I stood weakly and started to follow Will. When he headed toward the stairs, Alastair said, "Oh no, Will. You can talk here at the next table."

Will stood stone still for what couldn't have been more than a few seconds. It seemed like an eternity. Finally, he said, "Fine," and we sat two tables down from Alastair. By then we had attracted the attention of the bartenders and every other patron in the establishment. I could feel all eyes on me as Will started to plead his case.

"Why are you doing this?" he said. "No one will ever love you as much as I will. You know that. I know we've had some tough times, but I love you and I can't let you walk away. We're meant to be together. You can't leave."

"I am leaving, Will," I heard myself say in a voice as brittle as shattered crystal. "The paperwork has already been filed. I suggest you consult an attorney, and don't do anything foolish. It's over. I've finally had enough."

After a long silence, he abruptly stood and turned over the table, throwing it to the floor. I thought it was over for me. His next move would be to pull a pistol out of his pocket and shoot me in the forehead. Except for Wilson yapping inside his travel kennel, the whole bar hushed, and time stopped. Finally, he slapped a chair, tipping it onto the floor as he turned and stormed out of the bar.

I was trembling so badly after he left that I had to hold my drink with both hands. Alastair assured me I was safe, that he wouldn't dare try anything now with so many witnesses. All I knew was I had to get away.

A few minutes later, I waved good-bye to Alastair as he boarded his flight to Cleveland, and I walked to the American Airlines gate and caught the last flight of the day bound for LAX. When I fastened my seat belt and got Wilson settled beneath me, I panicked.

As the pilot throttled the plane away from the gate, I was consumed by fear. I just knew that Will had to be on the plane, somewhere behind me, waiting to pounce once we were airborne. I mustered enough courage to turn around and scan the passengers behind me, but I still wasn't convinced. Maybe he was hiding in the bathroom, or maybe he had slipped away on an earlier flight and was waiting outside my condo door in Palm Springs. Fear overwhelmed me. My heart raced, and I broke into a sweat. I couldn't catch my breath for a moment, and when I finally did, I called the flight attendant and begged to get off the plane.

"I'm sorry, ma'am, we're in line for takeoff. Is there anything I can get you?"

"You can get me off this airplane!" I shouted. Then I began to hyperventilate. The chief cabin attendant was called forward, and after a brief consultation with the captain, the plane returned to the gate amidst a chorus of groans from the rest of the passengers. Trembling so badly I could barely stand, I picked up Wilson and exited the plane.

"Are you going to be all right, ma'am?" the pilot asked as I waited for the ramp to extend.

"Once I get off this plane, I'll be fine," I said, but I didn't believe it. I thought I saw Will everywhere I looked. He was waiting behind the next corner or behind the closed door of the hotel room I rented for the night. I couldn't escape him. He would find me. I knew it.

✦ ✦ ✦

The events of that year were so painful, I pushed them back into the recesses of my brain. Will became a phantom. If I didn't think about him, then the torture I endured didn't really happen. That didn't stop the nightmares, though. For over a decade, I would wake up screaming for him to stop hitting me. When I became fully awake, I would once again repress the memories, so I wouldn't have to relive a moment of that time. I had been foolish to marry Will, but the price I paid for my foolishness was steeper than anything I imagined.

Immediately after filing for divorce, I traveled to Hartford, Connecticut, where the PGA Tour was hosting the Hartford Classic. I sought out Bobby and told him everything. He wrapped himself around me like a blanket, and we were together from that moment on. Four months after filing for divorce from Will, I married Bobby Cole in a Methodist church in Cape Town, South Africa, one week after Bobby had won the South African Open. Finally, my life was on track. The bad movie I had been trapped in for three years was over, and I could move on to grand things with a great guy who would never beat me, never pull any weapons, never threaten my life.

And there was the alcohol.

CHAPTER 8

MESSAGE
IN A BOTTLE

NOT ALL PROBLEM DRINKERS use alcohol as an escape mechanism. A fair number start out as moderate social drinkers who aren't trying to run away from anything. They live productive lives, concealing their disease from those around them. Perhaps the most famous is Betty Ford, the former first lady, who stunned the public and many of her closest friends when she confirmed her battle with alcohol.

Betty always appeared to be fine, a picture-perfect first lady, but her family knew of her problem, as is true of many families of those suffering from addiction. Her subsequent therapy at Bethesda Naval Hospital led her to create what is now recognized as the premier treatment center for substance abuse: The Betty Ford Center in Palm Springs. Certainly it would have been easier for Betty to internalize her problem and deal with it as a private family matter, but thank God she didn't. Because of her openness, people began to realize that alcoholics aren't necessarily those who visibly show signs of impairment. Betty championed awareness and opened people's eyes to the fact that alcoholism isn't always out front and in-your-face. Alcoholics are normal people like the ones you see at home and at work every day. They don't always fall as dramatically as I did.

For most people the signs are subtle—overdoing it on more than a few social occasions, one more for the road too many times, the need to drink on a regular schedule. For me, however, the triggers were anything but subtle, and my drinking was evident to everyone who came in contact with me.

After burying the Will Ross experience somewhere in my brain, I thought I finally had my life in order. I played in fifteen events in 1981 and had six top-twenty-five finishes, including a third-place finish at the Mary Kay Classic. By year's end, I was sixty-second on the money list—not great, but a reasonably respectable year by most standards. But by then my priorities had changed. I was anxious to become the tour wife I had dreamed of becoming when I strode the fairways of Augusta National watching Bobby in 1976. The second chapter of my life was upon me a little late, but here nonetheless. I was ready for an old-fashioned, traditional marriage where my husband was the primary breadwinner, and I'd support him by being a homemaker, a mother, and a good wife. I would work part-time, at least for awhile, but once the babies came—and I wanted them to come by the bushel—I would stay home. As popular as the idea of the working professional woman was in the 1980s, I didn't buy it. I wanted the same thing from my marriage that my mother had wanted from hers. I had made one horrible mistake already, and I wasn't about to do the same thing again. I entered my marriage to Bobby with as much gusto and fervor as I put into my golf game. This time, life was going to work out.

Four months after marrying Bobby, I found out I was pregnant. We were in Pinehurst, where he was playing in a tour event, and I took a home pregnancy test. We were both ecstatic, but I was torn trying to decide when I should stop working. There were tournaments I had committed to play and corporate outings I had promised sponsors I would attend. I had to make another trip to Japan in the fall. I decided to continue working throughout the pregnancy, but I would stop the minute the baby was born.

Things didn't work out that way. My playing golf didn't seem to cause any problems at all, and I even caddied for Bobby in San Antonio at the Texas Open just before departing for Japan. Then on the transpacific flight home from Tokyo, five months pregnant and ready to begin my life as a mother, I started hemorrhaging. When I arrived at home, I went to the hospital where the doctors gave me the bad news.

"Ma'am, I'm sorry, there is no heartbeat. Your baby has died, and we need to take it," a young internist said to me.

"Ma'am, I'm sorry, there is no heartbeat. Your baby has died, and we need to take it," a young internist said to me.

I refused to hear it. I got up off the examination table and said, "My baby is not dead. I saw his heartbeat right before I left for Japan. You're wrong, and I'm going home."

They had to be wrong, I told myself. I couldn't have lost this child that I so desperately wanted. During my high school days, I worked out and ran five miles a day during a time when women didn't push themselves athletically the way they do today. As a result, my body fat dropped so low that it affected my cycle, and Mom instantly jumped to the conclusion that I couldn't have children, a theme she harped on for years. Finally, she took me to the UCLA Medical Center, and because having sporadic periods was unusual even for world-class runners at that time, I was told that the likelihood of my having children was slim. Those doctors had been wrong. I had gotten pregnant almost immediately after marrying Bobby. Now, I was sure that these doctors were also wrong. My little boy was not dead, and I was going home.

Within hours I had a miscarriage. After returning to the hospital for the D and C, I was devastated. I cried for a week. Work had caused this, I was sure of it. If only I hadn't played so much, or traveled so much, my baby would have lived. It was my fault, and I began to question what kind of mother I would make if I couldn't even care for a child before he was born.

I didn't really have time for grief and self-doubt. Against strict doctor's orders, I became pregnant again two weeks after my miscarriage. This time I took no chances. The minute we got the good news, I stopped work until after the baby was born. It was the first time I had been completely away from golf, and the break did wonders for my attitude. On July 23, 1982, in a birthing center in Dunedin, Florida, with Bobby, my mother, and a midwife in attendance, I gave birth to a beautiful little girl. We named her Chelsea after the character Jane Fonda portrayed in the film *On Golden Pond*, and she was the light of my life. For all my expectations about parenthood, nothing really prepared me for how I felt when the midwife placed the small, crying new life into my arms. Tears filled my eyes, and a wave of change passed over me. It was no longer a concept or a dream; I was now a mother, and life would never be the same.

✦ ✦ ✦

While the time away from golf did wonders for my outlook, it did little for the family checkbook. Throughout the 1981 and 1982 seasons, Bobby played the PGA Tour with limited success. He made a total of twelve cuts in two years and brought home $35,549 in twenty-four months. A lot had changed since 1973 when that would have been more than enough money. Now we were a couple with an infant, a mortgage, and travel expenses. It costs a lot of money to travel from city to city every week, paying hotel, restaurant, airline, and rental car bills, as well as a caddie's salary. Those are expenses that are due whether a golfer makes one dollar or a million, and even in those days, $20,000 a year was the minimum a golfer needed in order to break even. In 1981 I made $21,034 in official earnings before endorsements, and in 1983 when I returned to the tour to play in thirteen events, I finished second at the J&B Classic and ended up with $34,029. Bobby made three U.S. cuts in 1983 and won $5,837.50.

When we began dipping into savings, I became concerned. Somewhere in the back of my mind, I remembered Bobby proudly recalling how many times he had been down to his last dollar, fighting to make a cut for enough money to check out of his hotel and get to the next town. That kind of hand-to-mouth pressure gave him a rush, as if being one putt away from destitution somehow made him more romantic and compelling. I wasn't impressed. The stories scared me. What was so grand and noble about starving?

I had grown up in Olive where the richest guy in the neighborhood was the dime-bag dope dealer, so I found nothing romantic about living on the edge of financial disaster. It concerned me that my husband didn't share my worry or sense of urgency when it came to getting his career back on track. I wanted to retire. By 1983 I had spent my decade on tour, and it was time to become a full-time mom. But now that wasn't possible. Bobby lost his exemption after the 1983 season. Then his wrist started hurting. After he rested at home until his wrist had plenty of time to heal, his elbow began to bother him. More time at home. Then his knee went out. When I suggested he might want to consider another job in the golf industry, teaching maybe, his response chilled my blood.

"Sorry, Laura, I'd love to, but I can't."

He used the exact phrase…the same words, in the same order, with the same inflection…that he had used that night in Orlando when I confronted him with the marriage ultimatum. Those words had haunted me for years, through my marriage to Will, my miscarriage, and through the birth of our daughter, and now the same sentence came out of his mouth again. *Oh, my God*, I said to myself. *He expects me to support him. He has no intention of going back to work.*

After 1983 Bobby never played the PGA Tour again with any regularity. He would occasionally gain a sponsor's exemption to an event, and every so often he played a mini-tour tournament when it was convenient and close to home. But as far as advancing his career as a playing professional, or as a teaching professional, or as anything professional under the sun, he chose to pass.

"Sorry, Laura, I'd love to, but I can't."

Once again I felt the pressures and anxieties that had plagued me throughout my professional career. It wasn't enough that I hadn't won a tournament, or that I had been criticized by my peers on tour for what they perceived as overt commercialization; now I had a family to support. No staying home and caring for my baby, no walking the fairways with the other tour wives, and no second life waited for me at the end of a rainbow. I had to work full-time to support my child and my husband.

Bitterness didn't seep in right away. Injuries in our profession come with the territory, and everyone, even the greatest players in the world like Nicklaus and Palmer, have lean years. My problem with Bobby was his cavalier, "cared for" attitude toward our impending downward spiral. Rehab for his various injuries involved sitting on the couch in our living room and surfing through channels on the television. When I suggested that he set up a regimen and begin working on a comeback, he would say, "I'd love to, but I can't. Right now I'll just sit here and rest." When it became evident that he wouldn't be playing the tour again, I urged him to seek other forms of employment. "I have a job," he would say. "I'm just recovering from an injury."

"Sorry, Laura, I'd love to, but I can't."

Those injuries varied from the elbow to the knee to the wrist, on again and off again for years. If he had chosen to become a ditch digger, I would have been the proudest ditch-digger's wife in the country. Instead, he chose to be cared for, just as he had been cared for by a cadre of servants while he was growing up in South Africa. Only now, I was the servant. The duties of wife and mother continued unabated, but I also had the added responsibility of earning all the family income. "I can't earn money as easily as you can, Laura," he would say. "The press loves you, and the sponsors love you no matter how well you're playing. I don't have that luxury, and I never have."

But the interest of sponsors and the media began to wane. My fifteen minutes of fame (which had stretched to almost a decade) ran its course when a young girl from Texas named Nancy Lopez burst onto the scene in the late 1970s. With Nancy winning tournaments left and right, I was relegated to the agate type in newspapers. The Japanese still held a loving fascination for me, and I still collected healthy endorsement fees from some overseas ventures, but for the first time in my life, more cash was flowing out of the coffers than was flowing in. My nest egg was still comfortable, but as the sole provider for the family, I had to consider how long I could continue to generate the income I had in my Ultra brite days. How was I going to have the tribe of kids I wanted if I had to keep working? My mother never worked outside the home a day in her life, and that is what I expected when I became a mother, even if it meant paring back my lifestyle. In order to do that, I needed Bobby to get off the couch and do something—anything—to contribute to the family. "Sorry, Laura, I'd love to, but I can't."

✦ ✦ ✦

When the situation with Will had become too much to handle, I popped the cork on a bottle of wine and fled into my own reclusive world. Doing it all over again was easy. At first I thought a change of scenery would offer the fresh start we needed. Bobby had become despondent. Wearing a perpetual frown, he would sleep late, don a pair of jeans, and plop himself, unshaven, on the living room couch where he would remain all day, every day. We both needed something to shake us up and get our minds and bodies in gear again. I sold our house in Dunedin, Florida, and we moved back to the California desert where I bought a condo at Ernie Vossler's La Quinta Resort. Mom moved in with us to help with Chelsea while Bobby and I got our careers back on track. To my dismay, after the boxes were unpacked and the furniture arranged, Bobby resumed his position on the couch. Frustrated and angry, I adjourned into Laura's World with a bottle of champagne and a Shar-Pei puppy named Chardonnay.

At that time alcohol was my way of calming my anger toward Bobby. He had, in my view, broken our contract, and I resented him because of it. Discussing our problems didn't seem to do much good, so I drank. In fact, everything got a little better when I drank. My workouts were more intense and more vigorous, my runs were more fun after a drink or two. My housekeeping improved with a drink in my hand, as did my cooking, my golf, my disposition, and my intellect. I was smarter, healthier, and happier with a snoot full of the good stuff. I didn't have to think about my long-term future with Bobby—the father of my child—a man I had loved almost from the moment I met him, who now appeared destined to spend the rest of his life glued to the sofa in a sitcom-induced stupor.

At least my golf had improved. In 1984 and 1985 I finished in the top fifty on the money list and made more official money than I ever had as a professional. I still didn't collect any wins, but my stroke average was as low as it had ever been, and I retooled my swing to add length and consistency. I beat practice balls like a madwoman. Just as I had done as a child when the pain of my parents' breakup became too much to handle, I used golf as an escape from my problems. The rhythm of the practice tee, the repetitive nature of practice, and the instant reward and feedback golf bestows were more therapeutic than anything I could have gained through counseling. Each shot I hit put my troubles farther and farther behind me, and before long I had two roads that led straight to Laura World: golf and the bottle. As long as I balanced them, I never had to leave the personal retreat I had created for myself. Golf, then drink...drink, then golf. I had it covered.

✦ ✦ ✦

By the middle of 1985, Bobby still hadn't gotten off the couch. When I suggested he get a teaching job, he responded, "Sorry, Laura, I'd love to, but I can't." I snapped. If he wasn't going to work, I wasn't going to support him. I had just passed a milestone, turning thirty years old on May 31, and it was time for me to take stock of my life. My first decision as a thirty-year-old woman was to tell Bobby he could waste away as a couch potato somewhere else. I'd had enough. Papers were filed that summer, and we were divorced in late 1985, much to the surprise of everyone in golf, who still had us pegged as the perfect couple. There was no question that I still cared for Bobby, but I couldn't stay married to him. It was the same lethargy I'd seen when he wouldn't get out of bed to meet me at the Augusta airport. I found it unacceptable then, and it was unacceptable now. Others in his life might continue to pamper him, but I wasn't going to facilitate it any longer. I

An apple a day...? I'm waiting to tee off in the middle of the first round of the 1985 Boston Five Classic. Rumors swirled around this time that I was anorexic, but I wasn't. I was just living off a diet of alcohol, mostly wine—which might explain my fondness for apples. (AP/WIDE WORLD PHOTOS)

moved into another condo a few miles away with Chelsea and my mom.

After Chelsea was born, Mom moved with us every time we changed addresses, and her advice never stopped coming, whether I wanted it or not. The moves seemed quite natural for Mom. She didn't work, so the role of grandmother gave her a renewed sense of purpose, which she embraced with all the vigor she had displayed fighting for women's lib and girls' golf teams. I love Mom, and she did a wonderful job helping me once I became a mother. But during those difficult times, I didn't need one more reminder of how I'd wasted my talent and screwed up my personal life. I reminded myself every day.

After the divorce was final, I treated myself by buying a new red Porsche 911, the ultimate in conspicuous consumption for a thirty-year-old winless professional in the throes of an identity crisis. I continued to drink. Wine had grown on me, and it still made all my other obsessions— working out, cooking, socializing, and playing golf—better. If I went out, wine was always part of the agenda. It was a magic potion that made me a more self-confident conversationalist. With a drink, I was a sophisticated, worldly, experienced thirty-year-old woman who had done well as a professional athlete. Without it, I was a girl from Olive with two divorces to her credit.

Booze helped numb the pain from an inexplicable void I felt in my life. Even though I had achieved more in my thirty years than a lot of people did in a lifetime, I felt an empty expanse in my soul. I had tried to fill it with golf, then marriage, then wine, but nothing seemed to work. I tried spending my way out of loneliness and depression, but even a new white Jaguar to go with the Porsche didn't help. Neither did the late-night parties I attended or the various men I met. What was wrong with me? I had a beautiful daughter and, even after my heartbreaking loss in Costa Mesa in 1986, a life that most people couldn't imagine. I played golf for a living! I'd never had to work in a factory, never been laid off, never had to scrounge for spare change to buy a hot meal, and never faced eviction, repossession, or even a rejected credit card. I lived in beautiful places, hobnobbed with important and well-heeled people, and because of all the work I had done early in my career, I still had a fair amount of money in the bank. My career was far from over, so what on earth was I missing? I didn't have the answer, but I knew something was missing from my life, and I had no idea what it was or how I could find it.

I went looking in all the wrong places. In 1988 Bobby came back to me with proof that he was a changed man. After I had hoisted him off the couch with divorce papers in 1985, he decided there might actually be virtue in work, not to mention a paycheck or two. He played the Canadian PGA Tour in 1986 and 1987, along with a number of U.S. minitour events. When he returned to California, he proudly boasted that he'd made over a hundred thousand dollars in tournament income, more than I had made with my golf clubs over that same period. This was a sign of redemption. Bobby had seen the error of his ways, and he was prepared to step up and be the provider I had hoped he would be. Certainly this was the missing link, the source of the emptiness in my life. Bobby was a new person now. This time, I knew things would be different.

✦ ✦ ✦

Bobby and I were remarried in an Episcopal service in California, and on June 12, 1988, I gave birth to our second child, a boy, Eric James (E. J.). I played golf through April 1988, and I learned that if I stretched properly and took care of myself, there was no reason I couldn't play golf well into my third trimester. It was a lesson that would serve me well later on. Now with two kids and two California residences, I wanted to finally capture that elusive stability I'd been searching for throughout my adult life. Perhaps that would fill the void. A little more structure and a real-life family life had to be what I had been missing. Surely, two kids and a working husband would bridge the emptiness that I felt inside. If that didn't, what could?

When E. J. was three months old, we sold both La Quinta condos and moved back across the country to a house in Orlando so I could be near my dad and both of my brothers. It was a wonderful time. Bobby played the Ben Hogan Tour, a PGA Tour–affiliated minitour that later became the Nike Tour, and I took the rest of 1988 off. By 1989 I had resumed working, although my pace was a little slower. I played in fourteen events in 1989 and fifteen in 1990, and gave birth to Haley in April 1990. That was the year my worst fears were realized. The man who had made a hundred thousand dollars in two minitour seasons while we were divorced suddenly rediscovered the couch after we moved to Orlando. This time the children were his excuse. Who would look after the kids? I was playing well enough to earn at least one top-ten finish every season, and as long as I was playing, sponsors continued to offer perks and

Most good golfers serious about staying sharp or improving their game spend a lot of time on the practice range beating balls, and I was no different. This is spring 1987, and I'm in La Quinta, California. (Laura Baugh)

endorsement opportunities that kept the money flowing in. "I can't earn money like you can, Laura. I'd love to, you see, but I can't." With four mouths to feed, I resumed a grueling LPGA Tour schedule in hopes that I could somehow, some-day earn one victory in between motherhood, housekeep-ing, and my duties as a wife.

Like an old friend, the bottle called me every day and every night. When I would walk out of my bedroom and see the back of Bobby's head sticking up like a periscope from the couch, I headed straight for the wine. No need to argue or create a scene. I knew without looking that Bobby's feet were on the coffee table and the television remote was firmly implanted in his palm. There was no reason to speak to him.

I anticipated his excuses before they came out of his mouth. Laura World awaited in the refrigerator. I could cook, clean, fold laundry, play golf, work out, and entertain the babies with a blood-alcohol level so high I was probably flammable.

In the morning I was supermom, and at night I was the super female. Another pregnancy came just fourteen months after Haley's birth. The moment I learned that I was having another baby, the drinking stopped. Just like that I put the wine and champagne away and didn't touch another drop. That's how I knew I wasn't an alcoholic. I took care of my body during all my pregnancies, and that meant no alcohol, no caffeine, and plenty of exercise and prenatal care. Alcoholics didn't do any of that. Alcoholics drank right up to delivery and their babies were premature, underweight, and malnourished. My babies were all healthy and happy, and I was a sober, well-adjusted pregnant woman. I loved being pregnant. For those nine months that a child was growing inside me, I knew the meaning of life, and the void I tried to fill with alcohol was filled instead with a new, growing, kicking life totally dependent on me.

I played golf throughout my fourth pregnancy. I had no other choice. We still operated on what accountants call "negative cash flow," where more cash was flowing out than flowing in. What endorsements I still enjoyed were contingent upon competing on the LPGA Tour. If I didn't play, we were in financial meltdown. I played in sixteen events in 1991 and seventeen in 1992, and I had a top-ten finish both seasons. But my game wasn't what it had been. I had six top-twenty finishes and my best financial year ever in 1991, with $70,920 in official earnings. Although my stroke average kept creeping up, my position on the money list kept sliding down. A new generation of players, including Laura Davies, Dottie Pepper, Brandie Burton, and Liselotte Neumann, had taken the LPGA Tour by storm. As I approached the twenty-year mark as a professional golfer, the questions about my ability, my drive, and my life decisions seemed to grow by the day.

My son Robert was born on March 13, 1992, and the cycle began anew. Bobby couldn't work, of course, because we now had four kids. He stayed home and changed diapers. I left my babies to go compete against women almost half my age, and the void filled with baby Robert returned with a vengeance.

Like an old friend, the bottle called me every day and every night.

The path to Laura World was set in stone. Rather than deal with my problems, I drank. Within a couple of months, I was back on a diet of wine in the morning to help me get out of bed and drinks throughout the day to make the problems go away. My IQ went up when I drank, and once more, I became Venus, a goddess of sensual allure. In March 1993, I found I was pregnant again, and in November of that year, my third son, Michael John, was born in Orlando.

I never touched a drop of alcohol during that pregnancy either, which reconfirmed my earlier delusional conclusions that I couldn't possibly have a drinking problem. Again the void had been filled with a growing fetus. My self-worth and identity seemed to be wrapped up in my ability to have children, a horrible reason to get pregnant. I was blessed with a crop of healthy children, who have been wonderful gifts regardless of my offbeat mind-set at the time of their conception. I am vehemently pro-life, but for some reason during that time, I assumed that "Go forth and multiply" was specifically targeted to me. But after each child's birth, the familiar void in my life returned, and I hopped right back into my drinking. Only this time I made up for the nine months I'd been sober, pouring more alcohol into my body over the 1993 holidays than I normally would in a year.

My worsening state of denial and substance abuse came as a culmination of a lot of forces, not the least of which was our declining financial situation. Before my marriage to Bobby, I had accumulated a healthy retirement fund that, assuming I could remain financially flush during my peak earning years, would carry me for the rest of my life. As the kids kept coming, and Bobby stayed home on the couch, those funds steadily dwindled. My bitterness toward him grew as it dawned on me that he had been living off the money I had earned before I ever met him. He couldn't work because someone had to care for our children. The problem was, I wanted to be that person. In hindsight I see that I was experiencing the same kind of identity crisis my mother had gone through. But rather than spreading my wings to carve my own niche, I set my goal to become a full-time wife and mother. I was the antifeminist who wanted nothing more than to be a homemaker. I was the mother and Bobby was the father. He was supposed to work every day, and I was supposed to care for the kids and keep the home. I played nine events in 1993 prior to Michael's birth, and my best finish was a tie for thirty-eighth. My stroke average ballooned above 75 shots per round for the second time in my career, and the paltry $3,482 I made on the LPGA Tour didn't pay for the diapers and formula I had to buy. My game was coming unglued when I needed it the most. With five children, three in diapers, pulling me in one direction, and the mortgage company pulling me in another, I followed my own path back to the refrigerator where a bottle of Chardonnay stood ready to whisk me away.

For the first time in my life, I felt that I couldn't stop drinking. After I celebrated Thanksgiving, Christmas, and New Year's Eve 1994, the alcohol in my system reached dangerously high levels, and I didn't feel comfortable stopping or even slowing down. I checked myself into the Sand Lake Medical Center in early January for my first medical detox. Dr. Johnson hooked me up with intravenous antibiotics, then chided me for getting myself into that kind of shape.

"Do you understand the dangers you put yourself in when you abuse alcohol this way?" he asked.

"Oh yes," I said, while thinking, *Yeah, yeah, just let me out of here so I can get home to my kids.*

"All right," he said. "These fluids will flush the alcohol out of your system, and I hope I don't ever see you again under these circumstances."

"Don't worry, you won't," I promised.

CHAPTER 9

*H*ITTING BOTTOM

I ALWAYS ASSUMED NO ONE knew about my drinking, because in my mind I was perfectly normal when I drank. My tolerance to alcohol was remarkably high, so I never considered myself impaired. When I went to Chelsea's school to meet with her teachers, nobody knew I had been drinking since before sunup, and nobody on tour suspected that I drank four or five minibottles of champagne before teeing off, or that I always kept an emergency supply of wine in my locker. In my mind, I had everybody fooled.

In reality, everyone knew. The women on tour would smell alcohol on my breath at eight in the morning, then roll their eyes and go about their business. The grocer knew, the druggist knew, the teachers, bankers, gardeners...everybody who came in contact with me knew I had been drinking. Few knew the extent of my addiction, but everybody knew I drank too much.

I missed the cut in nine of the first ten tournaments I entered in 1994, and many players said the pressure had finally gotten to me. There were rumors that my nerves were shot, that I couldn't finish a solid round. In part, the stories were true. If the pace of play was good, I could finish a round without any problems. But if play slowed, or we had a rain delay, I could only play fourteen or fifteen holes before I started shaking. Other players assumed it was nerves, but it was alcohol withdrawal. I was detoxing on the golf course. After a while my goal was to get as far under par as possible through the first thirteen holes, then try to hold off the shakes until I could get back to the clubhouse where a bottle was waiting.

Fortunately, the cycle was once again interrupted when I became pregnant with my sixth child, Evita Beau. By then, family and friends were openly concerned about my predictable patterns, not to mention the fact that six children seemed unmanageable for a working woman. From their perspective, every time I drank my way through depression, I would end up pregnant, and the drinking would stop. Miraculously, my golf game would improve, which led many sports writers to opine that I played better pregnant. They were right, but pregnancy had nothing to do with it. I played better when I was expecting because I wasn't drinking. While I missed three more cuts in 1994, I tied for ninth in the Youngstown-Warren LPGA Classic and competed successfully on several Florida minitours throughout my sixth pregnancy. Even more of a concern for my friends, however, was what would come after I gave birth. In the past, I had started back on the bottle right where I had left off, but the last couple of years those drinking episodes had become more intense, and my behavior had seemed more irrational. While the cycle was the same, the volume and magnitude of my drinking had increased dramatically. Those closest to me were afraid that after Evita was born, I would try to make up for lost time. A few of them, including my mother, voiced their concerns, but I completely dismissed them. In my altered state of thinking at the time, I knew I didn't have a drinking problem and those who thought I did were just misinformed. I deserved to drink. Anyone who juggled motherhood and a career as a professional athlete had earned an occasional nip or two.

By then the LPGA had established on-site day-care services for the mothers on tour, so the kids traveled with me from tournament to tournament. We looked like a gypsy caravan, but I had little choice. There were bills to pay, sponsors to satisfy, and six young mouths to feed. I couldn't expect Bobby or my mother to watch the children every week, even though neither of them worked, so the kids traveled with me and we became a media highlight every time we pulled into a player parking lot. "Laura Baugh, who travels on tour with her children in a van, has exchanged her status as the Ultra brite girl to one of Super Mom," one paper wrote. It was a consistent theme.

I led the tour in number of children—no one was even close—and my primary sponsor became Binney & Smith, the makers of Crayola Crayons. I presented the perfect family image the LPGA Tour should have been exploiting, but, for political reasons, avoided. Then, as now, the LPGA struggled with its image, primarily because of a battle between the professionals who wanted us to be just like the men on the PGA Tour and the professionals, like me, who thought it was important that we position ourselves as women and play to the female and family audiences. My ideas were not very popular then and even less so now. And the dark secret I had harbored for years was about to become very public. Mom and the rest of my family and friends had been right. Evita was born on

April 4, 1995. By May I was on a drinking binge that would almost cost my life.

✦ ✦ ✦

I rarely went out of the house to drink, which I know now is one of the first telltale signs of a drinking problem. I justified it by telling myself that I couldn't leave the children. I merited a drink, but unlike others who could go down the street to a local bar, I had to be home with the kids. Home life was a mess, and wine and champagne at the grocery stores were displayed on pretty little wooden racks next to the diapers, so it was very easy for me to snatch a bottle or two. It was even easier to stash them in my golf bag, my closet, my dresser, and my bathroom cabinets. Minibottles were the most convenient. Not only could I hide them in boots and the pockets of loose-fitting clothes (ostensibly to keep the children from finding them), but the portions were small enough that I could continue in denial comfortably. I consumed two or three liters at every sitting, but when it came in single-serving minibottles, what difference did it make if I drank six at a time? They were small, it was convenient, and I deserved it. But even that had become a self-serving lie I didn't truly believe. I had done nothing at the time to "earn" a drink, but as long as I continued to lie to myself, somehow it seemed okay.

After a few weeks, the shaking episodes came more often. I would wake up in the morning shaking so badly that I had to roll out of bed and crawl to the closet where a couple of minibottles had been hidden between my turtleneck sweaters and my socks. Trembling so badly that I had to use two hands to hold the tiny bottles, I gulped down the contents, sometimes chugging three or four of them in under thirty seconds. I had become adept at hiding my drinking from Bobby, even though he was in the next room. Of course, now I understand how co-opting his passivity was, but at the time I didn't care. I'd proven that I could get a drink whenever I wanted, no matter what roadblocks were in my path.

As far as I was concerned, the word *love* didn't come close to describing how I felt about wine. I worshiped it. The crisp bouquet coated my mouth, throat, chest, and stomach as the fermented fruits worked their way into my bloodstream and calmed my anxieties. It was everything to me. After throwing back a liter or two, I always took a deep breath as my heart slowed and my body relaxed. I could feel the trembling subside, starting with the larger muscles like my thighs and back and working outward until my hands were as steady as a surgeon's. Amazing. Not only did it let me escape the trappings of my personal situation, alcohol helped soothe my growing nervousness. It was better than hypnosis, and a lot cheaper than therapy. My pact with alcohol: Allow me to work out, hit balls, and play golf, and I'll let you help me with the little things in life like getting out of bed in the morning.

Alcohol didn't keep its end of the bargain. The shakes came calling more frequently, and my ability to work became more limited. In May 1995, six weeks after giving birth to Evita, I was scheduled to make a celebrity appearance at a breakfast meeting of the American Medical Association at the Orlando Convention Center. Meeting time was 7:00 A.M., which presented a problem. Most mothers of six might have trouble getting up, getting dressed, and getting the kids ready to make a 7:00 A.M. meeting, but that wasn't it at all. The problem was the jitters. At that time of day, I knew I would be trembling so badly that I couldn't possibly shake anyone's hand, much less speak. Alcohol had started to let me down. I couldn't work the kind of schedule I wanted. So I woke up at four and started drinking to calm my nerves. By six the shakes had stopped, and by seven I was smashed. The shakes were gone, but so was my ability to speak without slurring my words. That was okay, I thought. As long as I didn't shake, I could fake my way through the rest.

Somehow I maneuvered my van down International Drive in Orlando without killing myself or anyone else, swerving into the parking lot of the Marriott Hotel where I was meeting with several doctors, who were already busy discussing the latest medical breakthroughs. When the doctor who was coordinating the event approached me, I held out my hand to greet him. I meant to say, "Hi, I'm Laura Baugh," but something that sounded more like, "I, mm Lur Ba," came out of my mouth as I leaned back and forth trying to gain my balance.

At first the doctor didn't know what to say. My face was red, and even though I had downed half a tube of toothpaste and a dozen or so breath mints, I still smelled like I'd just come from a Napa Valley wine festival. He stared at me for a moment, then after I slurred my way though breakfast with a table full of physicians, the doctor in charge said, "I'm sorry, Laura, we really can't use you this morning. Can I call you a cab? You didn't drive yourself here I hope."

"Sure I drove," I said.

He insisted that I not drive home, so he called Bobby and had him pick me up in the hotel lobby. Embarrassed and ashamed, I made Bobby stop at the Publix supermarket. By then it was eight o'clock, and I knew that the stores had been open and selling wine for an hour.

Usually I divided my alcohol runs between Publix, Gooding's, and Albertson's, all large super-market chains within five minutes of my house. By splitting my runs among the three, I kept any single cashier or store manager from knowing how much I was buying. I bought mountains of toilet paper and frozen dinners, because I wouldn't dare buy only wine at that time of day. That was the sort of thing winos who camped out in front of liquor stores did, and I certainly was not a wino. Still, at eight, having been awake and drinking since four, I trotted into the Publix supermarket where I bought two frozen dinners and six minibottles of California Chardonnay.

Alcohol didn't keep its end of the bargain. The shakes came calling more frequently, and my ability to work became more limited.

By then the shakes had returned, and I needed to get a little more alcohol in my system for balance. Anxiety and paranoia overwhelmed me as I maneuvered toward the checkout line. I had to pay with a credit card, but my hand was now shaking so badly, I couldn't sign my name. When I got in line, the cashier didn't look up. She knew I was drunk. Why else wouldn't she look me in the eye? The credit card machine churned out a receipt while the girl smirked and bagged my wine on top of the frozen dinners. When the receipt finally finished printing, I grabbed a pen and I scribbled an illegible line in the signature space. Then I snatched my little soldiers and I marched out to the van where I downed two bottles before Bobby put the key in the ignition.

Suddenly my nerves calmed, my paranoid anxieties went away, and all the tension that had consumed me only seconds earlier disappeared. Once again I stared at my hand in amazement. I took a pen and a small notepad out of my purse and I wrote my name in perfectly legible, swirling, swooping script. No nervous scribbles, or ticks, or tremors. Amazing.

✦ ✦ ✦

A week later the family and I loaded up the van and drove to Myrtle Beach where I made my debut as a television analyst for the women's NCAA Championships. Although I drank throughout the telecast, I did remarkably well in the booth. So well in fact that the very next week, we traveled to East Lansing, Michigan, where ESPN had asked me to work their telecast of the Oldsmobile Classic. From the days of my show in Japan I had always loved television, and I thought this could be a milestone for a new career. Lots of players my age had adjourned to the broadcast booth, splitting their time between playing and commentating. At that stage in my career, it seemed like the perfect move. I still held name recognition with viewers, and I had enough television experience that my presence in the booth made perfect sense for the network. It would also be good for me. If things worked out, ESPN would contract me to cover a predetermined number of events for a set fee. I could then plan my playing calendar around the broadcast schedule. All I had to do was impress network producers and executives in Michigan. This was the break I needed. I had to do well in Michigan.

Of course, the added pressure I placed on myself sent my nerves into a frenzy. The prospect of a new job and new career hung in the balance. I needed to be at my best when I climbed into that ESPN booth, so throughout the trip I made Bobby stop every hundred miles or so for quick bathroom breaks. My bladder is small, but not that small. Every truck stop and gas station we visited ended up with a couple of empty wine bottles in the trash. I didn't overdo it. I drank just enough to stay on an even keel throughout the trip. As my nervousness increased, however, I began to mix the drinking with some postpartum depression medication prescribed for me after Evita's birth. I was supposed to take the medication instead of drinking, but since I knew more about my body than any doctor, I found a happy equilibrium between medication and alcohol.

We spent my fortieth birthday on the road to Michigan, Bobby driving while I did my best to keep the shakes to a minimum. When we arrived, Larry Cirillo, the ESPN producer who was in charge of the Oldsmobile Classic, escorted me to the tower where I would be working, and we walked through the procedures for the week. He was more than accommodating, and I did my best to put on a bright and happy face. There was a job on the line, and I had to do whatever it took to hold myself together for the week.

Things went remarkably well for the first couple of days. I got to know all the cameramen, producers, and technicians, and I meandered around the course, reacquainting myself with the layout and the nuances of this event. I took notes, talked to players, and did my best to prepare myself for two days of live telecast. As far as I could tell, no one knew I was petrified, drinking before, during, and after our rehearsals. On Friday, one day before we were to open the live telecast, the delicate balance I had found between post-partum drugs and alcohol suddenly evaporated.

We were in what television producers call (ironically enough) a dry run, a real-time rehearsal. Larry even inserted commercial breaks. By then I had overloaded my system. The shakes had been so bad before entering the booth, I drank a few extra bottles to wash down my medication. The shaking stopped, but I became disoriented. I fumbled with the IFB (the "interruptible feedback" earpiece that broadcasters use so they're in contact with the producers), and I plopped myself into the chair. When it came my time to speak, the words would not come out properly. "The guff is a difcut cuss cuss for hitting specialty the green," I mumbled.

"What?" I heard over my IFB.

They quickly went to someone else, but within a couple of minutes, I heard another of the announcers say, "Laura, what do you think about that?"

Jolted out of a stupor by hearing my name, I said, "Right, that's. It...I...good shuts."

What the hell had I just said? I didn't understand myself, so I knew there was no way anyone else had a clue what I was trying to convey. There was a palpable pause over the airways. Within a couple of seconds, the rhythm of the telecast resumed, and I tried to regroup for another shot. The least I could do was complete one cohesive sentence.

When Larry gave the signal to come back to me, my brain and my mouth weren't in the same body. I wanted to say, "She's got about 144 yards to the flag," but what came out sounded like, "Shits but hon fur yurd…flig."

That was it. Twenty minutes into the rehearsal Larry Cirillo pulled the plug and I was asked to leave the booth. Mortified and disoriented, I stood on wobbly legs and tried to maneuver my way down the narrow metal stairs. About a third of the way down, my bladder began screaming for me to hurry, while my inner ear was telling me to take it slow. I didn't look at the ground for fear of getting vertigo, but I knew that I had to get to a rest room as quickly as possible. I stumbled down the last four stairs, holding onto the thin handrail. I had been assigned to the fifteenth green, fully a quarter of a mile from the nearest rest room. My legs carried me quickly toward the clubhouse, but not quickly enough. As I stumbled through some high grass on the right side of the sixteenth fairway, my bladder released.

With my pants stained front and back, I slumped down and sat in the grass until a passing LPGA Tour official offered me his jacket and a ride back to the clubhouse. I accepted the jacket, then looked down and watched as my future in television drowned in a growing puddle of urine.

✦ ✦ ✦

I caught a ride from a courtesy car driver back to the Sheraton Hotel, but my condition only worsened as the alcohol and anxiety proved a lethal combination. My stomach lurched as I staggered into the hotel lobby, and I did my best to trot to the nearest ladies' room before throwing up.

In the handicap stall, I purged all the alcohol I'd consumed throughout the day, then I blacked out. Hotel personnel found me sprawled on the floor, soiled with my own vomit, and after going through my purse and determining that I was a guest, the manager called Bobby and respectfully requested we check out.

We left Michigan that afternoon and Bobby drove straight through to Orlando. Along the way I felt myself seriously detoxing. My heart rate and blood pressure skyrocketed, and when I wasn't hanging out of the window throwing up, I was slipping in and out of seizures. Bobby was afraid that I would die on some lonesome stretch of I-75, but when I was conscious, I assured him that I could detox myself. We stopped at various convenience stores where I bought wine coolers and slowly began bringing my alcohol level down by guzzling the less-potent drinks. Thankfully, the makeshift treatment worked, and we made it back home where, after stopping by the house to pick up a few of my clothes and a toothbrush, Bobby dragged me back to the Sand Lake Medical Center for yet another dry-out session.

This time Dr. Johnson wasn't as congenial as he had been the first time I overdid it. "I think we've been here before," he said with cold ambivalence.

"I know," I said. "It's just that I was going through some postpartum depression, and I had this television audition. It was just a mistake. I drank too much. It won't happen again."

I could tell by his cool response that the good doctor had heard that one a few times before. He left me in my room alone, hooked up to IV fluids. The shakes came and went and I felt like a colony of ants had been released over my body. The itching and tingling were almost unbearable, and my head began to pound with pain. I yelled at every nurse who came into my room, but they had seen and heard everything before, too. Nobody listened, and nobody cared. All I had done was drink a little too much while taking some medication. That was no reason to treat me like I was some sort of drunk.

Three days later when I returned home from the hospital, my mother and Bobby had searched the house and removed all alcohol from the premises. The structure would be alcohol free, they unabashedly told me, which sent me through the roof. Not only was I still irritable from three days of detox, but I had paid for that "structure" they were now deeming an alcohol-free zone, and if anybody was going to set the rules of the house, it was going to be me. I let Mom and Bobby know exactly how I felt in a less-than-civil and louder-than-normal tone, which scared the kids. They had never heard their mommy yell with quite so much vigor. I blamed Bobby for that as well. If he had just left me alone and let me drink a little wine, I would have been fine. Everything would have been fine.

I accepted the jacket, then looked down and watched as my future in television drowned in a growing puddle of urine.

I stayed alcohol free for almost a week, but soon I was sneaking over to my neighbor's house where I begged a drink or two and chatted away the afternoon. Then I would sneak out to the grocery store where I would buy enough minibottles to carry me until my next excursion. Sometimes I would drive home, park in the driveway, and sit in the car while I drank as many as six or seven minibottles of wine. Mom and Bobby knew that I had been drinking, but I didn't care. What they thought was secondary to my getting a drink. Besides, I enjoyed proving to them that they couldn't cut me off. I wanted an occasional drink and no one, especially not Bobby or my mother, was going to tell me that I couldn't have what I had rightfully earned.

Weeks turned into months, and I continued to drink as much as I wanted when I wanted. I constantly reminded Mom and Bobby, it was my house. The door was still in the same place it had always been, and they were welcome to leave anytime they wished. I was operating in and out of blackouts by that time, and I would sometimes go for long periods of time with no recollection of what had happened. It wasn't as though I had passed out, or at least I didn't think so. Of course I vomited quite a bit, but that was to be expected. I didn't eat much, except for the ice cream that helped lubricate the wine for its return trip up my esophagus. Vomiting became part of my new covenant with alcohol. Eat a little, drink a lot, throw up, and start all over again. The blackouts bothered me, though. Sometimes I would wake up not having remembered going to bed. A few times I was bruised, and when I asked Bobby what happened, he said that I had fallen or pulled something over on myself. Once while I was on the floor of my bedroom doing sit-ups, I inadvertently pulled over the television stand (I hooked my toes under for support), and the television landed on my head. That prompted a trip to the emergency room, but I refused to stay because I knew the nurses would run a blood-alcohol test, and I would be back in detox. I didn't even remember doing sit-ups, much less pulling the television over. It wasn't until I returned home and saw the broken television stand that it started to

I guess you could describe my mom, Sally Louisa Boyer-Baugh, as eccentric. Here she is with my nephew, Byron Hale Baugh, in 1992 while enjoying "brunch with Mickey Mouse" out at Disney World in Orlando. (LAURA BAUGH)

make sense, but I still couldn't recall what had happened. Time was a vacuum, and sometimes I would lose large chunks of memory.

After a while the episodes became too much for those around me. One afternoon, after I had established an acceptably high alcohol level in my bloodstream, I was standing at the edge of my pool rocking back and forth in an obvious state of pain-free inebriation, when my mother walked by and pushed me. I slipped on the wet tile and hit my head on the corner of the pool as I fell in. Mom then turned on her heels and headed back inside. If I died, so be it. She had seen enough. Although I'm sure she would now admit it was a mistake to leave me, Mom had a history of reacting badly to "situations." From the time she and Father began fighting in Cocoa Beach, to the fervor with which she took on her many causes in California, she always seemed to go over the top in terms of responding to whatever confronted her. I'd gotten used to it. During one of my earlier blackout episodes, Mom decided to cut my clothes off of me with a large kitchen knife. Ostensibly, this was so she could throw me into the shower, but when Bobby walked by and saw the knife, he shouted, "What are you doing?" When she explained, he replied, "Wouldn't unbuttoning have worked?" This time, he walked past the pool and saw me lying unconscious and drowning beneath six feet of chlorinated water. He dove in and pulled me to the side, but as he was giving me mouth-to-mouth resuscitation, Mom came out and said, "Let her die. She's determined to kill herself anyway."

Such was life in the Cole residence throughout most of 1995 and 1996. I drank all the time, detoxing myself with wine coolers when I needed to remain lucid enough to conduct some business; then I would sneak next door and hoist a few more with my neighbor. By then my face was a perpetual shade of red with blotches of pale scaly skin covering my neck and cheeks, and I had given up on concealing my drinking from anyone. I loved it too much to care. Everybody knew, but as I told my friend Marlene Hagge, "That's just who I am. I like to drink."

Shortly after the new year in 1996, Bobby had me admitted to Sand Lake for yet another detox, much to my displeasure. Dr. Johnson wasn't the least bit sympathetic.

Sure, I drank way too much, but I still paid all the bills and kept a roof over everyone's head, so it was nobody's business if I wanted to drink a little every now and again. The last thing I needed was this damn hospital, with its contemptuous staff. On the third day, the alcohol counselors came by the room with all their doomsday literature and substance-abuse lecturing…blah, blah, blah. All I needed was a good hot shower and a good cold drink.

Then Bobby came by, and we had words. He informed me that at home I would be on "restriction," a term he and Mom had concocted to mean "house arrest." There would be no phone calls, no car privileges, no alcohol, and no contact with the outside world. If I hadn't been lying in a hospital bed with IV tubes in my

I drank all the time, detoxing myself with wine coolers when I needed to remain lucid enough to conduct some business.

arm, I probably would have hit him. I was agitated enough, but it went far beyond superficial anger. I had been a prisoner in my own house before—in Argyle, Texas, where a madman had monitored my every move, taken away my phone privileges, and broken my contact with the outside world "for my own good." Now, I was being told that it was happening again. I wouldn't have that.

As soon as Bobby left the hospital room, I got on the phone and called a cab. Within minutes I had checked myself out of the hospital, and I was on my way to a friend's house where I showered, changed, and had a couple of drinks before heading home. If they thought for one minute that I would sit idly by while they locked me away in my own home, they all had another thing coming. I was in control, and as long as I continued to have a pulse and a will, I intended to stay in control.

✦ ✦ ✦

When I walked in the front door, all pretty and clean, Bobby and Mom flew into one of their ugliest fits yet. They ranted and raved and insisted that I was, as of that moment, on permanent, maximum-security house restriction. My car keys and credit cards were gone, and the phones had been locked away. I was to stay home until I conformed.

I nodded, smiled, and went into my bedroom where I grabbed a suitcase and began packing my clothes.

"What do you think you're doing, young lady?" my mother yelled.

"I'm leaving. Obviously, I can't make either of you leave, even though this is my house, so I'm going away for a few days."

"You're not going anywhere!" she screamed as she grabbed my suitcase and flung clothing all over the room. "You're staying right here until we say otherwise."

With that I stormed into the bathroom and locked the door. Mom and Bobby assumed that I was simply blowing off steam and that after I calmed down, I would come out and sheepishly accept the restrictions. But I had stashed one of my checkbooks under the towels in the bathroom cabinet for just such an emergency. I stuffed the checks into the back pocket of my jeans, and after listening through the door and determining that Bobby and Mom were on the other side of the house, I exited the bathroom and made a dash for the front door.

Our gardener was standing in my yard with a hose in his hand when I sprinted outside. "I need a ride and I need it right now," I said. At first he didn't understand, but when I said, "Hurry, I'll pay you, but I need you to drive me to the bank immediately," he nodded, rolled up his hose, and the two of us hopped into his car.

As we turned off my street and headed toward the subdivision entrance, I saw Bobby chasing us on foot. He had discovered I was missing and realized when he heard the gardener's car backfire that I was making a jailbreak. "Too late," I said in a sing-song voice as I gave a little mock wave in Bobby's direction.

✦ ✦ ✦

The gardener drove me to Barnett Bank where I sweet-talked a dumb young teller into cashing an obscenely large check without seeing my ID. My wallet with all my identification was under lock and key somewhere in the house, so I was going to have to make this escape on my charm and looks. So far, so good.

After I had enough money in my pocket to make a mugger's dreams come true, I had the gardener drive me to a fitness gym, where I bought a drink and called a cab. Ten minutes later, I was in Dillard's department store buying luggage, clothes, makeup, toiletries, and a purse while the cabbie waited out front. Properly outfitted for an extended stay, I adjourned to the airport where, once again, I had to charm an unsuspecting ticket agent into selling me a ticket to Arizona with no identification.

"My wallet is in the cab, and I'm about to miss the flight," I said. "I just need to pay cash for a first-class ticket to Phoenix. Please, hurry." The agent bought my lie about the wallet, and after a smile, a wink, and the "please," he printed my boarding pass, and I was on my way to the desert.

I chose Phoenix because I was scheduled to play a role in an infomercial for the Alien Wedge later that month, and the company had chosen Phoenix as the site of the shoot. Going out a little early, especially under the circumstances, made perfect sense to me, even though I was traveling without my driver's license or credit cards. Once in Phoenix, I put a large cash deposit down on a hotel room and proceeded to the bar where I ordered a glass of the hotel's best champagne. "So much for house arrest," I said to myself with a smile as I chugged the champagne in one gulp.

✦ ✦ ✦

I gave Bobby twenty-four hours to calm down before calling him with my whereabouts. He wasn't pleased, but after a few minutes of listening to him vent, I appealed to his most rudimentary instinct: money. "Bobby, you have to pack up my golf clubs and send my wallet out here. I have to practice if I'm going to play, and I have to shoot this infomercial while I'm out here. Without my clubs, I'm not much good to the infomercial people, and if I don't play and practice, I can't get paid." After another tirade, he finally bought the argument and sent my golf bag and wallet to Phoenix.

As soon as the package arrived, I rented a car. The infomercial had been postponed, so I decided to drive to

Palm Springs where I could practice in a comfortable environment (where I had friends) before returning to Phoenix. With a bottle in my lap, I drove west through the desert, pondering the events of the previous week and considering my options. How dare they treat me like a prisoner in my own home! When I left Dallas I had sworn I would never let myself be trapped like that again. Nobody was going to place me under house arrest now. When I hit the Palm Springs city limits, I checked into my favorite hotel in Indian Wells. After settling into my room, I phoned an attorney and began the process of filing for my second divorce from Bobby.

After watching him sit on the couch for a decade, I had it up to here. This time I wouldn't stand for it. I spent several hours on the phone getting the ball rolling and hung up with a drained feeling of accomplishment. This time I was leaving for good.

After hanging up the phone, I opened the minibar in my room and saw that they had no champagne and only two bottles of wine, but plenty of hard liquor. That was okay. I would simply pour the hard stuff into a wineglass. That way I wasn't really drinking straight vodka or rum. As long as it was in a wineglass, it had to be okay. I finished the entire minibar in an hour and called down to room service to have them restock it. After the attendant refilled the bar, I hopped into the shower, then, standing in my room naked, I polished off the second minibar in less time than it took to drink the first. "You're okay," I said. "As long as it's in a wineglass, it's okay to drink it." That was my last conscious thought.

One of the maids found me beside the bed. She quickly called 911, and when paramedics arrived at the hotel they couldn't find a pulse. I still had color, so I hadn't been down long, but the medical technicians needed to work fast. After several attempts at shocking my heart, they finally jump-started a pulse. When I woke up, I was strapped to a bed in the intensive care unit of a Palm Springs hospital.

"What's going on?" I asked.

"Just lie still, ma'am," a nurse said. "You gave us quite a scare."

I had no idea what she was talking about, and, quite frankly, I didn't care. I wanted to get up and go home. This time away had been fine, but now I had work to do, kids to feed, and places to be.

"I'm sorry, ma'am," a doctor said as he checked my chart. "We've had to Baker Act you for this incident."

"What's that?" I asked.

He told me the Baker Act was a California law that required anyone in danger of hurting him or herself to undergo three days of care and counseling in a managed substance-abuse facility. I didn't have time for such foolishness, and I told the doctor as much.

"You don't have a choice," he said without much sympathy. "It's the law."

Two days later I was escorted by the local authorities to the front door of the Charter Treatment Center, where I spent three days playing basketball and fuming over the idiotic law that landed me there. What were they thinking? I wasn't a danger to anyone, especially myself. I had six children for God's sake! What was I going to do, kill myself and leave six kids with no one to provide for them? Absolute lunacy! The evils of alcohol were drummed into my skull—again—and I was told that I had to recognize my

problems before I could help myself overcome them...
yada, yada, yada.

As soon as I was released from Charter, I took a cab to
the nearest grocery store where I bought a six-pack of bub-
bly. I drank two of them in the ladies' room before crawling
back into the cab and returning to the hotel. Once there I
thanked the housekeeper for saving my life, then I gathered
my belongings. Everything in my room was just as I had left
it except for my father's West Point ring, an heirloom that I
carried with me everywhere I traveled. The ring was missing. I screamed, cried, and vented in front of every manager
in the hotel, but to no avail. The ring was gone. As I got in
my rental car and sped back toward Phoenix my only
thought was, *What am I going to tell Father?*

✦ ✦ ✦

As tempting as it was to go straight home to Orlando
after the Baker Act incident, I still had a chance to earn
enough money to keep this trip from being a complete
boondoggle. The Alien Wedge people were setting up their
infomercial shoot to coincide with the Standard Register
Ping—a full-field LPGA event held at the Moon Valley
Country Club. With any luck, I could shoot the infomercial,
play in the Monday qualifier, and perhaps earn a spot in the
tournament.

True to form, I was too drunk to enter, so I went shopping instead. Then I lost track of time. Whether I blacked
out or simply stumbled around in a hallucinogenic stupor,
I ended up outside my Phoenix hotel room with blood
everywhere. At first I thought I'd been mugged. That was

what I told hotel personnel and the police. I had been shopping, and it seemed as though some packages were missing, but I really didn't know. A report was filed, but the police were skeptical. I was incoherent, babbling, and I had obviously been hitting the sauce pretty heavily before the alleged incident occurred. It didn't take a mental giant to conclude that I had staggered into a door or fallen on the street.

The infomercial hadn't gone through. I blew off the Standard Register Ping. My heart had stopped in a hotel room. I had been Baker Acted and forced to spend three days locked in a Charter treatment center, which resulted in the loss of my father's West Point ring. And to cap it all off, I had been mugged—or at least I thought I'd been mugged. The trip was an unmitigated disaster, so I grabbed another bottle of wine and drank myself silly as I waited for a flight to Orlando.

I'm not sure where and how I blacked out, but from what I have subsequently pieced together, I was completely unconscious in a chair at the Phoenix airport when a police officer strolled by and tried to wake me.

"Are you all right, ma'am?" he asked. When he realized that I was incoherent, he opened my purse and found my driver's license. After calling home and speaking with Bobby, the officer called an ambulance, then called the LPGA tournament office at Moon Valley. When I woke up, I was once again in the hospital, only this time I had a visitor. Mindy Moore, a former player who worked in public relations for the tour, was sitting at my bedside. The first words out of Mindy's mouth were, "Thank God, Laura, I thought you were going to die."

"Where am I?" I asked.

"You're in the hospital. I'm going to stay with you and fly you home."

After everything I had been through, the last thing I wanted was Mindy Moore chaperoning me back to Orlando. At the first opportunity, I sneaked away from Mindy, checked myself out of the hospital, and caught another cab to the airport. I booked the first flight back to Orlando, but when I boarded the American Airlines flight and attempted to order a drink, the flight attendant informed me that the airline was under strict orders not to serve alcohol to me.

"What?" I shouted as we pulled away from the gate.

"I'm sorry ma'am. Someone called ahead and instructed us not to serve you."

"No, you don't understand," I pleaded. "I know I drink way too much, but I just need a drink so that I'll be okay. Do you see how I'm shaking?" I held my trembling hand up for her to examine, but she seemed unmoved. "All I need is one drink to calm my nerves. I don't fly well anyway. You can monitor me. Please, just one drink so I'll feel safe."

Nothing worked. After we were airborne, the plane ran through some turbulence, and I shouted, "Come on! I've got to have a drink. I'm dying!"

That prompted a very terse response from the chief flight attendant, who informed me in no uncertain terms that I wouldn't be served. If I insisted on disrupting the flight, I would be restrained and placed under arrest when we landed in Dallas. As much as I wanted to scream and claw somebody's eyes out, I sat on my hands and bit my lip for the remainder of the flight.

We had a one-hour layover in Dallas, and I hit every bar between my arrival and departure gate, downing a minimum of three drinks in each establishment before trotting off to the next watering hole. I needed to drink enough to get home, assuming they wouldn't serve me on the second leg of the flight either. By the time we took off, I was sailing free and easy, and when we landed in Orlando, I hit two more bars between the arrival gate and baggage claim. When I finally made it home, I stumbled on the door stoop, falling on the tile floor of my foyer and losing my luggage across the room. "Oops," I said with a giggle. "I'm home."

✦ ✦ ✦

Seven weeks later, May 17, 1996, a brown-eyed internist with a serious countenance looked at me very solemnly as I lay strapped to the bed in the intensive care unit at Sand Lake. "We're going to do everything we can to help you, but you need to prepare yourself and your family for the possibility of the worst," he said.

Death. He was talking about death...dying...checking out. Leaving my kids behind. This was no joke, no scare tactic, and no syrupy substance-abuse counselor telling me how awful it was to drink. This was the real thing. My head continued to swell and my hands looked like roadkill. I wanted to cry, but my eyes wouldn't tear because of all the blood that had seeped from the sockets. "Oh, my God," I said to myself. "I'm going to die a drunk."

My mother came and wept at my side. "I love you," she kept saying between sobs. "Oh, God, I love you so much."

She stayed by my bed through the first twenty-four hours, crying and preparing herself for my imminent departure from this earth. Then Mom left for a few hours and returned with the children, giving each of them a chance to say good-bye before Mommy's internal organs erupted into her bronchial tubes and she drowned in her own blood.

The youngest were scared of me, and I can't say I blamed them. All of the ugliness I had displayed in my actions was suddenly manifesting itself physically. I looked like a ghoul, with dried blood and inflated welts all over my body. I told each of the kids how much I loved them, but my words rang hollow. How could I leave them like this if I truly loved them? What kind of an example had I been? What sort of life had I really led? "Oh, Chelsea, E. J., Haley, Robert, Michael, Evita, I'm sorry to hear about your mother. How did she pass away?" "She drank herself to death," would come the response in unison. What on earth had I done to myself...to my kids...to everyone around me? Once the tear ducts began working again, I cried until I was completely spent.

I looked like a ghoul, with dried blood and inflated welts all over my body. I told each of the kids how much I loved them, but my words rang hollow.

Then the shakes came. Had I not been strapped down, I'm sure I would have fallen off the bed from the seizures. But this time I was wide awake, coherent, and totally aware of everything and everyone around me. After the seizures, the vomiting came, and I was sure that was the end stage. At any moment I would go into convulsions, then cardiac arrest, then flat-line death. I kept waiting to hear the buzzer on the heart monitor, wondering if I would still be conscious after my heart stopped, and for how long. Relatives and friends sent flowers, so at least I would die with a proper floral arrangement. A nurse tried to give me some water from a cup, but I couldn't get the straw in my mouth because of the shakes. When she finally was able to insert the straw and I pulled the cold liquid into my mouth, I instantly threw it back up. Nothing would stay down. This was it. I knew it.

Much to my surprise, I was still alive the next day, and the day after that. I still wasn't out of the woods, but my platelet count hadn't dropped any lower, and there were signs that it might be picking up. I had lost so much weight that the restraints, which had been painfully tight when I first arrived, were so loose that I could slip out from beneath them if I needed to stretch my legs. I was pale, gaunt, thin, scabbed, and a swollen ugly mess, but at least they had cleaned off the blood. My father and brothers had come to visit, as had my good friends Mark and Betsy McCormack; and even though we had some serious moments, we'd had a few minutes of levity as well. Mark asked if John Tolson, a local minister and spiritual counselor for many athletes, could come by and spend some time with me. "Sure," I said. What could it hurt?

At the end of day three, the doctor returned with some news that took my breath away. "I've never seen anything like this," he said, "but your platelet count is moving back up at a remarkable pace. It just passed 150."

"You mean I'm going to live?" I asked.

"It looks that way, yes," he said. "You're a very lucky woman, Laura. I hope you realize that."

I was so overwhelmed I couldn't answer him. For some unknown reason, I had been given a reprieve—a chance to look death squarely in the face and walk away. By all rights I should have died, but I didn't. I was recovering. My platelets were shooting skyward, and my body was bouncing back.

"It's a miracle, Laura. Make good use of it."

The next day, Reverend John Tolson showed up at my bedside. After introducing himself and spending a few minutes talking about my condition and the remarkable way I had been spared from death, he asked the question I had been waiting for.

"Laura, are you ready to accept help?"

"Yes," I said, tears streaming down my swollen cheeks. "Yes, I am."

CHAPTER *10*

I AM NOT IN CHARGE

To THE SURPRISE OF DOCTORS at the Sand Lake Medical Center, my condition continued to improve. When my platelet count rose to 170, it became clear I was ready to be released for the time being. Possible liver damage would be assessed later. At that moment, though, the most important thing was to get me into a program before I killed myself or injured someone else. Physicians at Sand Lake had done all they could. Now it was up to professionals in the field of addiction to save me from future calamities. After my admission to John Tolson, Mark McCormack, who had been a major part of my life since he signed me as a seventeen-year-old client, took charge, and within hours I was booked at the Betty Ford Clinic in Palm Springs. An hour or so later, my brothers had packed a bag for me, and John stood at my bedside ready to escort me to California.

Everything had happened so fast. As I weakly pulled on a pair of jeans and slowly stretched my aching muscles, John told me that we would be leaving for the airport within minutes.

"I need to go home and shower before we go any-where," I said.

"That won't be necessary," John said.

"What do you mean? Look at me." Swollen and discolored, I still looked like a character out of *Tales from the Crypt*. "I can't get on an airplane looking like this," I said.

"You'll be fine, Laura," John said in a soothing voice. "I'll be traveling with you. As much as I know you want to go home, we need to move you straight into Betty Ford. They're expecting you tonight."

I was too weak and light-headed to put up much of a fight. I had bled out and stood on death's door for four days, and I looked it. All I wanted was a hot shower and a little makeup, but John was insistent. Later, I learned that nobody wanted me to return home, even for a minute, for fear that I would either grab a drink from my stash or that I would orchestrate another elaborate jailbreak. Those fears were probably well founded. While I had admitted to John that I needed help, I still wasn't ready to admit that I was an alcoholic. Sure, I had trouble drinking too much, and I needed help controlling my behavior, but I wasn't a dirty ole alkie. I still couldn't force myself to accept the truth. I knew I would die if I didn't get help, but I didn't know if I could see myself as a drunkard...a wino...a gutter-crawling boozer who couldn't control herself. I was too scared to admit the truth and too weak to put forth the lie that had landed me in the hospital in the first place. Death scared me, and I knew if I took one more sip, I would probably die. But the thought of being a drunk scared me as well. Confused and tired, I accepted the fact that before the end of the day, I would be in California.

My family said good-bye as an orderly pushed my wheelchair out the front door of the hospital. Waiting outside, my brother Beau opened the door to his car, and he and John helped me into the backseat. Good to his word, less than an hour after signing the release papers at Sand Lake, John Tolson was sitting next to me on an L-1011 bound for Los Angeles. Five hours later, still looking like I was at the end stage of some strange jungle virus, I wobbled through the LAX terminal and out to a car that Mark McCormack had arranged to pick us up. John put my bag in the back, opened the door for me, and the two of us headed south to Palm Springs.

A little before 9:00 P.M., we pulled into the parking lot of the Betty Ford Clinic. By then I felt much better, even though I hadn't bathed in four days and my hair was falling out in clumps. John and I laughed as we recalled the stares in the airport and on the plane. "I'm sure they were hoping it wasn't contagious," I said with a nervous laugh.

It all seemed surreal. John took my bag and we walked through a cluster of trees and down a back-lit cobblestone path. I felt a little like Alice in Wonderland as we wound through the darkness. From what I could see, the place seemed well manicured, but as we approached what appeared to be a low-rise building, I found the ambiance strange and a little spooky. I slowed down when I saw a shadow walking toward us.

"Mr. Tolson?" the figure asked.

"Yes!" John shouted. The figure finally came into view, and I could see that he was a distinguished man with a charming smile.

"You must be Laura," he said, his hand extended.

"Yes," I weakly muttered.

"We've been expecting you." The man took my bag from John and left us alone for a minute to say our good-byes. I thanked John for everything he'd done (although it scared me that he was leaving me with this stranger) and I gave him a weak hug. Then I turned and followed the man down the path and into what appeared to be an office building.

Other than for the two of us, the entire building seemed to be empty.

"We need to get you registered. Everyone else has turned in for the night," the man explained.

"Can I get something to eat?" I asked. It had been a long day and I hadn't had dinner yet. Four days of throwing up everything in my system had finally caught up with me. I looked anorexic and I felt that I could eat fifteen pizzas in one sitting. A twenty-ounce porterhouse with a salad, baked potato—butter, no sour cream—and a side vegetable would have been nice.

"The kitchen is closed," he said. "But I'll see if I can get you a sandwich."

◆ ◆ ◆

Because of the way I looked and the humiliation I felt at being there in the first place, I checked into Betty Ford under the alias Laura Boyer, my mother's maiden name. I was quite taken with my cleverness. Nobody had to know that I was in treatment but me. I could slip through the system unnoticed, or so I thought. It took about two days for everybody in the world to know what had happened to me and where I was. I even received flowers from fellow tour players. My big secret couldn't have gotten out faster if I'd posted a notice on the Internet. Still, that first night I needed to protect what little dignity I had left, so I lied about my identity as I scarfed down the very thin ham sandwich the administrator slapped together.

After signing the necessary paperwork in the first building, the man led me back outside, down another dark pathway, and into a second building. This one seemed more clinical, more like a hospital, than the first building. A woman in a white coat took my bag and escorted me into a glass cubicle with an empty metal table in the center. "Are these your belongings?" she asked.

"Yes, but I have no idea what's in there. My brother packed for me, and—"

Before I could finish, the woman had poured the contents of my bag onto the table and was sorting through shampoo and nail polish. She started two neat but distinct piles. "This can stay," she said as she put certain items in one pile. "But this has to go."

I needed to protect what little dignity I had left, so I lied about my identity as I scarfed down the very thin ham sandwich the administrator slapped together.

When my hair spray went into the "has to go" pile, I said, "What are you doing?"

She didn't look up from her sorting as she answered. "I'm taking out anything that has alcohol. Mouthwash…certain types of perfume…hair spray…anything like that."

"Hair spray?" I asked.

"That's right."

I couldn't imagine anyone drinking hair spray, but I soon learned that many alcoholics will drink anything—rubbing alcohol, almond extract—and yes, some even pierce aerosol hair spray cans and mix the liquid contents with soda water or 7-Up. I learned that recovering alcoholics refer to those desperate acts as "yets," meaning you might not have done it "yet," but that didn't mean you wouldn't. Everyone at Betty Ford had a "yet" story, including me. Just as I couldn't imagine drinking hair spray or shampoo, other people couldn't fathom a petite professional athlete mixing ice cream with Chardonnay, or detoxing herself with wine coolers. We all had our dirty little secrets, and once we started sharing with each other, we all understood. The drug could make you dance to whatever tune it chose. It didn't care who you were, or what you did for a living, or how rich or poor you were, or whether you were black, white, or polka dot. Alcohol was an equal opportunity destroyer. As I watched in stunned amazement, the woman in the cubicle picked out every item that could possibly tempt me to the next level of "yet."

Then she started asking questions. "How often do you eat? What do you eat? How much do you eat when you eat? What do you drink when you eat? What do you drink when you don't eat? What's your favorite drink?" The questions went on for about twenty minutes, even though I had no idea why such trivial information was important. Who cared what I ate or how many meals I missed? I thought this was alcohol treatment.

Finally, after asking all sorts of seemingly useless questions and confiscating my hair spray, mouthwash, shampoo, and a few makeup items, the lady ushered me down a corridor, beneath a breezeway, and into another building that had the look and feel of a dormitory. "You're lucky," she said. "You get to stay in the Swamp."

That had an ominous sound to it. "Swamp?" I asked.

"Yeah. All the rooms here have two beds. Every patient has at least one roommate, except for the Swamp which has four beds and two baths."

"You mean I'm going to be in a room with three other people?" I asked incredulously.

"That's right," the woman answered. "It's really an honor. When Betty first went into treatment at the Bethesda Naval Hospital, she was put into a room the navy called 'the Swamp' with three other roommates. She was the first lady of the United States and she was being asked to share a dorm room and a bath with three other women. When she balked a little, the naval officer said, 'I'll see if we can't move the other ladies out for you, Mrs. Ford,' but Betty said, 'No, they need this just as much as I do.' She said it turned out to be one of the best experiences of her life. So when she built this facility, she added the Swamp in honor of her own experience. Now, you get to stay there."

It was a nice story, but I wasn't overjoyed by the prospect of three roommates, especially given my current appearance. Other than my family, the last time I'd had a roommate was in 1975, when Donna Caponi and I decided to split travel expenses by rooming together. That had worked out fine, but after twenty years of having my own space, I didn't feel at all "lucky" now that I had roommates. The three other women in the Swamp were even less thrilled by my presence. When the administrator showed me into the tasteful but spartan room and introduced me to the others, a palpable chill settled over the small space. I'm sure they thought I'd wandered in off the street. I mumbled a greeting as I quietly laid my bag on the vacant single bed in the corner and scanned the room for a telephone. There wasn't one.

"Where's the phone?" I asked.

"The rooms don't have phones," the woman said. "You can use the phone on Saturday."

I nodded and said goodnight. Five minutes later I leaned against the fiberglass wall of the small shower and let the hot droplets of water pound against my chest, neck, face, stomach, and legs. It was the most wonderful shower of my life. As I dropped my chin to my chest and rolled my head from side to side, letting the cleansing, pulsating stream run through my hair and down my back, I thought again about the telephone. I never went a full day without talking to the kids, and I usually called them four or five times a day. I should have called home the minute I arrived. Then there was the way the woman had answered my question. "You can use the phone on Saturday," she had said. Today was Friday, so why hadn't she said, "You can use the phone tomorrow"? It seemed an odd answer, but so far everything had been odd. I was in a place where people drank hair spray. Nothing would have surprised me.

I don't require a lot of sleep anyway, but if I got thirty minutes of REM sleep that first night in the Swamp, it was an accident. I lay awake staring at the dark ceiling for hours, listening to the strange and scary sounds coming from my roommates. Two of the women were heroin addicts who hadn't completely detoxed, and the moans, groans, whimpers, tears, and nervous pants they uttered throughout the night were disconcerting and sad. At first I was frightened, then after a few hours I wondered how many times I had made those same noises during blackouts. I was no different from any of them. In some respects I was probably worse. They hadn't spent the last four days clinging to life in a hospital bed, nor had they spent the last year fumbling in and out of blackouts, fighting nosebleeds, concussions, and low platelets. We were all there for the same reasons. As that fact slowly dawned on me in the darkness of that first night, I was saddened by the agony my roommates were going through, and I felt a kinship to them. "It's okay," I wanted to say out loud to them. "I've been there. I know."

✦ ✦ ✦

Everyone got up at six and we all had breakfast together. The food was wonderful—lots of fresh fruit and healthy breads—but when I asked for regular coffee, I got another rude awakening.

"Sorry, ma'am, there's no caffeine in here."

The breakfast room server nodded, reinforcing the fact that, indeed, caffeine was forbidden in Betty Ford.

"You mean I'm here for twenty-eight days and I can't have any caffeine?" I asked.

The nodding continued. "No salt either," he said.

It took a moment for that to sink in. I had already detoxed from alcohol, so the withdrawal symptoms from my drinking were almost behind me. Caffeine was another story. I drank almost as much coffee as wine, and going an entire month without a caffeine jolt seemed unthinkable. Later I discovered that if I drank twenty-eight cups of decaf without a rest room trip, I got the same rush as from one cup of high-octane java. Once an addict...

After breakfast we were expected to go outside and trot around a quarter-mile track. Weak and frail, I slowly walked around the path alone. The sores had scabbed, and I felt a little better, but my appearance scared the rest of the patients. Some of these people were hard-core drug users—a tough bunch to scare—but I was such a grisly sight, no one wanted to come near me.

After our walk we started structured meetings. The first was a lecture where we all sat in an auditorium-sized room and listened as a counselor walked us through the reasons we were there and what we could expect from our twenty-eight-day stay at Betty Ford. Then he started talking to our group about our problems.

"To varying degrees, all of you have surrendered control of your life to alcohol or drugs," he said. "At first you didn't admit it, and you may not be completely admitting it to yourself now, but the fact of the matter is, you have lost the battle with the drug. It is trying to kill you, and, so far, you have let it succeed."

I looked around at the people sitting next to me and wondered if they were as struck by the words as I was. It was like he had been following me for the past year and knew everything I'd done, everything I'd said, every lie I'd told, and every blackout I'd suffered.

"You tell yourself you're in control, that you can handle it. It's no big deal. Just one more hit—one more drink. You deserve it."

Yes! Yes! Those were the exact thoughts—the exact words—I had used. I deserved it. Drinking was my reward, my trophy that I hoisted above my head after a long grueling battle. How did he know? How could this total stranger know my most intimate thoughts? This wasn't some twenty-year-old graduate student giving a sing-song lecture on the evils of drinking. This man knew what it was all about. He knew the raw detail, the rationalizing and justifying. He didn't call us by name, but he knew who we were, and he knew what we thought. I sat up a little straighter and listened more attentively. I was starting to get it.

We broke for lunch at noon, then reconvened in smaller group sessions. My early afternoon group consisted of fifteen people, some of whom had drinking problems and others who suffered from various drug addictions. One girl had become addicted to prescription painkillers, another was a mainline heroin addict. I was the worst-looking member of the bunch, and my hair came out in clumps every time I ran a brush through it. But after a few hours, the others began warming up to me. Each of us took turns telling our stories, recalling the first time we abused drugs or alcohol, the last time we drank, and the worst times in between.

Each of us took turns telling our stories, recalling the first time we abused drugs or alcohol, the last time we drank, and the worst times in between.

From that group I learned that blackouts were common, as were the shakes, the all-night binges, throwing up, mixing drugs, and making irrational decisions. Drinking on the job was a given, as was lying to everyone around you. Each story prompted collective nods from the other members of the group. We had all been there. The details were different in everyone's case, but we all shared certain unmistakable similarities. We all loved our drug, and we would do almost anything for it. In my case I jeopardized my career, my family, even my life for a drink of cold, crisp, sparkling champagne. Nothing was more important. I loved the way it smelled, the way it tasted, the way it tickled my tongue and bounced down my throat. I loved the way it made me feel, the way it made me look, act, and speak. There was nothing about drinking I didn't love. Even the bad things weren't so bad when you considered how wonderful the good stuff was. The seizures weren't so hot. The shakes and the insomnia had become something of a pain, and the inability to work had put a real strain on the family cash flow, but that was just the price I had to pay, the price we all had to pay for our drugs. No one was shocked or even surprised by the stories I told. Wetting myself after falling apart in a broadcast booth...vomiting and drinking coffee so I would be sober enough to visit my daughter's school...detoxing myself on the road...losing time in the desert...the mugging...the airport blackout...the hotel where my heart stopped beating. As I told these stories, everyone nodded. Everyone knew.

✦ ✦ ✦

Our days were very regimented: up at six and out to breakfast, then the walk (which I turned into a run after two weeks of gaining my strength back). Meetings began promptly at 8:30 and ran until 12:00. An hour for lunch, then more meetings, usually in smaller groups. From 3:30 to 4:30 you could work out in the on-site gym, which I did regularly, but at 4:30 we all went back to meetings. Individual sessions, one-on-one with a counselor, usually took place between 4:30 and 6:30. Then dinner and more meetings until 10:00. It took a few days to get accustomed to the regimentation, but after some adjustment I loved the structure, the discipline, and the fellowship that kind of environment offered. The first day was tough, especially when I realized why the woman who checked me in and sorted my belongings had said, "You can use the phone on Saturday," instead of, "You can use the phone tomorrow." Saturday was the only day of the week you could receive or make any phone calls, and then it was only for a few minutes. That was a huge adjustment for someone who talked to her children as long and as often as I did, but I soon filled my phone withdrawal with letter writing. I wrote every child a letter every day—six letters a day for twenty-eight days, a total of 168 letters. Visiting day was Sunday, but the only visitors were Bobby, Chelsea, and my mom as part of the family therapy program. It was just as well that no one else came. I needed that time to expel the demons that had taken up residence in my body and to finally, after years of searching, fill the void that had plagued my life for the better part of three decades.

It took quite a bit of time, even after going through Betty Ford, for me to admit, once and for all, that I was an alcoholic. For the first week I wanted to continue the lie: I had trouble drinking, but I wasn't really an alcoholic. A little adjustment and I would be able to control my behavior. I drank too much, but I certainly wasn't a drunk. It took a jolt for me to realize I was deluding myself, and God provided that shocker early in my second week.

During one of our small-group sessions, a young woman, probably twenty-five or twenty-six, told the story of her drinking. She started out as a casual "pretty" drinker. It was social—cool—the hip thing to do, especially among her peers. She was more popular when she drank, so she turned up the volume on her alcohol consumption until she was drinking all the time. Of course she made all the promises: "never before 5:00 P.M.…never before lunch…only one before breakfast…never after midnight." Like a good alcoholic, she broke them all and before she realized what had happened, she was drinking every two hours, fighting the shakes, and living in and out of blackouts. It was during one of those blackouts that someone…she had no idea who…took advantage of her sexually and infected her with HIV. As she sat with us, she was in the end stages of full-blown AIDS. Her demons had cost her everything. She was going to die awake, alert, and aware of everything she had done to cause her ultimate demise. This wouldn't be a blackout death. She would die sober and alone.

The story was a dagger through my heart, in part because of the tragedy of this young girl's life, but also because in almost every detail, it was my story. I could have recited nearly every word she had shared, because I had been there. I had been the sexy, pretty, popular drinker who found life a lot more interesting after downing a bottle or two. I had gone to the edge where I had watched the blood pour from my body—where I had purged everything from my system—and where I knew that death was mere minutes away. But I didn't die. My weight and strength had picked back up as my appetite increased. My blood work had returned to normal. My liver turned out to be damage free, despite my best efforts to destroy it. I would go home from Betty Ford to my six loving children. This girl would never read her own children a bedtime story, never sing a lullaby, never mend a torn band uniform, or kiss a fresh boo-boo. She would never cry with her daughter or cheer for her son. Her story had been my story, but in my forties I would go on living; she in her twenties would die. It could have happened to any of us.

After our session together, I returned to the Swamp where at lights out I drew my legs in close to my body and cradled my pillow next to me as I wept. Each tear fell like a weight.

During my morning session the next day, I heard the words I had heard every day since arriving, but for the first time they took on new meaning. "You are not in control," the counselor repeated for the umpteenth time. This time I really listened and I began to understand. "Your life, everything you do, is in the hands of a higher power. Sure, you believe you're in control, but you have a higher power inside you that controls your destiny."

"A higher power." What did that mean, exactly? When I put forth that question, the response surprised me.

"Everyone has a personal interpretation of what 'higher power' means," I was told. "But those of us who have suffered through substance abuse know, beyond a shadow of a doubt, that our lives are beyond our control. We place our trust in a higher power, and we have to live our lives one day at a time."

She was in the end stages of full-blown AIDS. Her demons had cost her everything. She was going to die awake, alert, and aware of everything she had done to cause her ultimate demise.

I played those words over and over in my mind, and I tried to reconcile them with the fact that I would live while the girl in our group session would die of AIDS, probably before her thirtieth birthday. Was it random? Could meeting this girl at this time in this place have been a coincidence?

Luck? An alignment of the stars? That just didn't make sense. There had to be a message in the life that would end and in mine that would be spared. What was it the doctor at Sand Lake had said? "It's a miracle, Laura. Make good use of it."

Make good use of it. I searched my soul for the answer. How was I supposed to make good use of it? What was I supposed to do? Who was I to deserve a miracle while others were destined to die? What had I done to earn a second chance?

When the epiphany finally came, it was like scales falling from my eyes. God had saved my life, had given me a new chance and hope for the future, and He had put me in the Betty Ford Clinic at the same moment as this poor child with AIDS to understand "the miracle" I had been given. This didn't come easily for me. While I had always considered myself a God-fearing person, I never took my beliefs to the next level. On this earth I knew I was in control. I thought about God, but I never prayed much, never considered the possibility of a Grand Plan for my life or for the lives of those around me. I had always been a control freak, probably because I was never in control. Mom had taken me away from Father without so much as asking my opinion. Will had beaten me to within inches of my life and I continued to stay with him. My marriage to Bobby hadn't turned out the way I had planned, so I drank. The signs were all around me, but I had been too caught up, too self-absorbed, too drunk to notice.

I wasn't in control.

Once again, I buried my head in my hands and I wept uncontrollably as I purged all the sorry, sorry actions of my life. The wasted years, the misguided energies, the foolish egotism. It all fell out in a blubbering crying fit as I sank into an emotional tizzy. All the lies I had told and all the people whose feelings I had hurt rolled through my mind like spirits, and I sobbed until I could no longer stand. That was it. As I finally took the long sobering breaths that follow such a cleansing cry, I felt the answer in my soul. The void had been filled, not by alcohol, or sex, or superficial materialism, but by the one thing I had been missing in my life: my higher power, which I called God.

◆ ◆ ◆

Answers don't always come as quickly as we would like, especially after decades of bad decisions and misguided behavior. Throughout the remainder of my stay at Betty Ford, I had to reconcile myself to the fact that my alcoholism was an incurable disease but one that I could control by never drinking again. I also had to come to the realization that most of the problems I encountered in my life were of my own making. I could not control what others did when I drank, and I would not be able to control what others did now that I was sober, but I could control my own actions.

My response to whatever situation I found myself in was totally and completely within the boundaries of my control. In learning that lesson, I had to admit many mistakes. I couldn't control my parents' bickering, nor did I have any say when my mother moved me to California, but I certainly had control over my reaction to that situation. Even at that age, I had self-will, and some of the choices I made were wrong. I certainly didn't make Will Ross beat me, but I had the power to respond in a proactive way to his assaults. I chose not to do it. Instead, I rationalized, internalized, and drank.

Likewise, I could never force Bobby to stand up to his responsibilities as the father of our children, but Bobby never made me drink. I drank because I opened a bottle, poured the contents in a glass, and chugged away. There is no other reason, and blaming others or hiding behind the "escape" excuse serves no purpose but to deflect attention away from what is clearly my responsibility. I behaved poorly for a long time. God willing, those days are behind me, but I have to recognize that I am not in control, and I never will be. My life is in God's hands, and the two of us are taking it one day at a time.

To the shock and dismay of many members of the LPGA Tour, along with my friends and family, shortly after my release from Betty Ford, I became pregnant with my seventh child. There was a great deal of speculation that I had fallen back into the same destructive cycle and that after my pregnancy I would go straight back to drinking. There was also more than a little head scratching at why someone with six children and dwindling bank accounts would bring another life into this crowded world. These were all valid concerns, but in my heart I knew that the child was God's gift, and that my sobriety would hold throughout. I was right on both counts. Jamie Lee Cole was born on August 27, 1997. She came into an alcohol-free family on the road to recovery and, God willing, she will grow up to know that her mother has a disease, but that through fighting that disease, her mother sets an example for other mothers who have troubles they think they can't overcome.

During my seventh pregnancy, the media attention I received skyrocketed once again. Now I wasn't the siren of the LPGA Tour or the Golden Goddess of Golfdom, but a recovering alcoholic and a working mother of soon-to-be seven. While my first instinct was to withhold some of the more gruesome details of my ordeal, I remembered the message I'd learned in California. I had been spared for a reason, and perhaps that reason was to share my story with others so that everyone would know it's never too late, that you can change, and that as long as you are breathing and your heart is pumping blood, there is meaning to your life. In June 1997 I got to share that message in a venue I never thought I'd see again. In East Lansing at the Oldsmobile Classic, I was leading the golf tournament at seven under par in my seventh month of pregnancy with my seventh child. Larry Cirillo, the same man who had been forced to pull the plug on me as a broadcaster at the same event, asked if I would come into the booth for an interview. It had been a long trip since I had babbled my way out of a television career in that same city, but when I entered that ESPN booth and spent a couple of minutes telling the world my story, I felt another weight had been lifted. The next day Larry came by the range and told me how proud he was of my recovery. My journey was far from complete, but each day I took another step; and in Michigan I took a step that went a long way to building my confidence as a recovering alcoholic.

✦ ✦ ✦

No one is promised an easy road, even after turning your life around for the better and doing what you know in your heart to be right. My life hasn't been a bed of roses since I found sobriety. In terms of my health, I'm in better shape now than ever, which, in and of itself, confirms the miracle. The fact that I am, according to my doctor, "as healthy as a twenty-year-old," is a blessing I can't explain. My golf is another story. In 1998 I played in fifteen tournaments, made eleven cuts, and finished no better than tied for thirty-fourth. Certainly the pressures of working through my disease, caring for a new baby, and sorting out life played a big part in my lackluster performance, but, once again, the blame is all mine. I didn't play well because I took time to get to know my children again. When I first came out of Betty Ford, I spent hours looking at them. It had been so long since I'd seen them through clear eyes, and I wanted to spend time reacquainting myself with each of them. As a result, my golf suffered, but I wouldn't change a thing. If I had won five times on tour and lost touch with my children, none of what I had gone through would have mattered. I now know the odds of my winning on the LPGA Tour are longer than they have ever been, but I also know that I have seven people at home who couldn't care less. If I had a room full of trophies and no one to share my life with, I would have nothing. My children are my life, and when I play today, I carry a beeper. If there is an emergency, I withdraw from whatever event I'm playing in and attend to my first priority.

That's how I refer to my children now. They are, without question, my top priority and my reason for being. But there was a time not too long ago when I acted in ways that proved otherwise. Alcohol came first, with God and family falling somewhere farther down the list. I certainly convinced myself I was a good parent, but you can't be a good mother while you're drunk. Passed out on the couch does not qualify as being home for your children, and drinking before breakfast doesn't win you any Mother of the Year awards. When I was in the worst stages of drinking, like everything else, I lied to myself and to everyone around me about my parenting. Being the oldest child by six years, my first daughter, Chelsea, was more aware of my drinking and more adversely affected by my behavior than any of my other children. Not that any of them escaped unscathed. During my episodic adventures E. J., Haley, and Robbie were all old enough to know that something very bad was going on, but they had no idea what it was.

Passed out on the couch does not qualify as being home for your children, and drinking before breakfast doesn't win you any Mother of the Year awards.

Once I took the first steps toward recovery, I sat each of them down and explained, as best I could, what had happened and why I had behaved with such callous disregard. Most non-addicts can't comprehend how a mother could do some of the things I did, but just like the crack addict who will do almost anything for the next fix, I was so consumed by my drug that nothing else mattered. It was beyond foolish. My judgment was impaired and my parenting suffered. I have apologized to each of them and they now travel the road to recovery with me. It is a never-ending journey, however. My relationship with my children continues to evolve, and we all continue to grow. Michael, Evita, and Jamie Lee are still too young to completely understand everything that happened, but they all know their mom has a disease she will battle for the rest of her life. As they mature, I will explain my alcoholism to each of them in as much detail as they need to understand. Every day I pray that none of them is afflicted as I am, but by being open and honest about what I've experienced, hopefully I can save them the agony.

It's been tough for Chelsea. She grew up with the burden of a mother who staggered around the house in a drunken fog most of the time. For the first six years of her life, she was an only child who traveled with me and played at my side while I was working on a golf career. During her formative adolescent years, a time when she needed me most, I would occasionally feel guilty during moments of lucidity, but rather than taking Chelsea aside for some much-needed quality time, I would purge my guilt by taking her to the mall, stopping to have wine at more than one of the restaurants in the mall. The more I drank, the more money I spent, trying to buy forgiveness from my daughter.

Chelsea was fourteen years old and at the precipice of womanhood when I entered Betty Ford. She needed a strong female influence, a role model for the first steps into adult life, but when she needed me the most I was struggling to stay alive. My poor daughter was forced to fend for herself during those years, and she struggled through my alcoholism as much as or more than I did. Chelsea came to Betty Ford for the family therapy sessions, at which point the counselors did their best to prepare her for the road ahead. The true victims of alcohol abuse are the children who stand witness to the devastation going on around them, and Chelsea was no exception.

For months after I returned home, we were like strangers. Rightfully bitter for what she perceived as selfishness on my part, Chelsea remained guarded about our relationship. Even when I opened up to her, I didn't feel the connection that I had hoped would come. In fact, it took over two years to mend the frayed bonds with my daughter. During that time we spent hours together, talking about everything—boys, food, the future; if it came to our minds we would talk about it. These sessions usually occurred at night, after I got the other kids down for bed. I would lie down in Chelsea's room and we would talk about whatever was on her mind. We would laugh and cry and talk about the things that mothers and daughters share only with each other. During one of those sessions, as I was passing the two-and-a-half-year milestone of sobriety, Chelsea said, "Mom, I want to tell you that I never respected you when you were drinking. You weren't somebody I could look up to or even talk to. Now, it's like you're a different person. I love you, but more than anything, I respect you now." It was one of the most touching moments of my life, and one that I will always cherish.

Chelsea never gravitated toward golf. In fact, she doesn't play at all. The golfers in the family (so far) are my oldest son, E. J., and my second daughter, Haley. They can't wait to get out on the course every day. The two of them have inspired me to play golf like never before. When I'm home, E. J. and Haley run home from school so that the three of us can slip out to the golf course for a quick round before dinner. When school is out for the summer, they can't get enough of the game, just like my brothers and me when we were young. Now I know how my father felt taking Hale,

Beau, and me out for the cod fish matches every afternoon, and I appreciate how tough it must have been for him when I was no longer a part of that foursome. Having my children with me on the course gives me a new and healthier perspective on golf.

It's wonderful having the kids with me when I'm out on tour and, in that respect, I'm very lucky to be a professional golfer. My kids travel with me during the summer. Unlike many working parents, I have the luxury of a full-time nanny who helps out while I'm working. Plus, the LPGA Tour, in conjunction with Smucker's, provides on-site day care at every tournament for the professionals who have small children. It's a great arrangement. The older kids follow me during the tournament rounds while the younger ones are only a few yards away in the tournament day care. I can't think of another profession where a mom of seven could take her kids to work, but, fortunately, that's how I work.

Not that there aren't problems. Moving my crew out requires a great deal of effort, and scheduling has always been an unyielding task. A minor miscue in our family schedule can have a devastating domino effect. If one child is fifteen minutes late getting in from swimming classes, it pushes the trip to the pizza restaurant back a half hour, which then throws another child's rendezvous with a friend off by a good forty-five minutes. Because of those problems, our household exists on a rigid timetable where promptness is paramount. Golf taught me the importance of scheduling at an early age. Whether you are forty years old or ten, tee times are inflexible. You're either on the tee ready to play at your appointed time or you're disqualified from competition. No second chances, and no excuses. So from the time I

It's ten days till Christmas 1998, and a sober mom shows off her wonderful brood.
(LAURA BAUGH)

was old enough to play competitive golf, I learned to organize my time and stick to an uncompromising schedule. With seven kids, those skills have proven invaluable. We are all up at a certain hour, with an allotted time for showers and breakfast, then off to school, work, and other activities. I return to cook dinner, clean the house, wash and fold a seemingly endless mountain of laundry, bathe the kids, check their homework, and get everybody ready for bed. Typical stuff for any working mom. I just happen to play professional golf for a living.

I also attend to these duties as a single parent. Unfortunately, the problems in my marriage lingered after sobriety, and in December 1998, I officially filed for divorce—again— from Bobby Cole. Certainly, I was never the best influence on Bobby, but like everything else in my life, I had to come to grips with what I could and what I could not control. Divorce was not my first choice, but it soon became a necessary part of getting my life back in order. It makes life harder, especially with seven children, but through my greatest adversities have come my greatest strengths, and my bond with the children has gotten stronger since the divorce. I firmly feel that it is a blessing in disguise for both me and for Bobby.

I played until my eighth month of pregnancy with Jamie Lee, then, after giving birth, I returned to the tour for sixteen events in 1998. My performance wasn't what I would have hoped (my best finish, a thirty-fourth, came at the Weetabix Women's British Open), but I looked at the year as a growing experience, a chance to get my life, my children, and my body back in shape. A large part of my schedule these days is a workout regimen that has improved my strength, my flexibility, and my stamina. As a result, I'm in better shape now than at any other point in my life.

My relationships on tour still need some work. Because I operated as a black-out drunk, there are still a great number of blanks in my memory. I've apologized to everyone I can find for the things I might have done or said during those times, but I'm sure there are many people to whom I owe a heartfelt "I'm sorry." The problem is I don't remember, so it's tough to offer enough apologies.

As for the future, I'm never supposed to speculate beyond the day that God has given me, but I'm playing better golf than I ever have in my life. I am in better shape than I've ever been, and nothing scares me any more. When you've listened for your own heart to stop beating, a five-foot putt for birdie is easy. Perhaps putting golf in its proper place in my life, behind God and family, has lightened my burden and helped me play better. In any case, I'm as capable of winning today as I ever have been in my life.

But whether or not I ever hoist a winning trophy above my head, whether I go down in history as a golfer who wasted tons of potential or as an athlete who overcame monstrous odds to finally prevail, as long as I draw sober breaths, I know I am a winner in life. That is the example I hope to set and the lesson I hope to teach anyone willing to learn. My life is a simple lesson, summed up in words spoken by the great Winston Churchill: "Never, never, never, never give up."

I live those words every day of my life, and in doing so, I hope I leave a legacy for my kids that extends far beyond anything I could possibly accomplish in golf.